CONTENTS

4 NATURAL

11 BOOMERANG

18 MACHINE

22 COOL OUT

29 BAD LIAR

36 WEST COAST

50 ZERO

45 BULLET IN A GUN

58 DIGITAL

65 ONLY

70 STUCK

76 LOVE

84 BIRDS

90 BURN OUT

96 REAL LIFE

NATURAL

Words and Music by DAN REYNOLDS,
WAYNE SERMON, BEN McKEE,
DANIEL PLATZMAN, JUSTIN TRANTOR,
MATTIAS LARSSON and ROBIN FREDRICKSSON

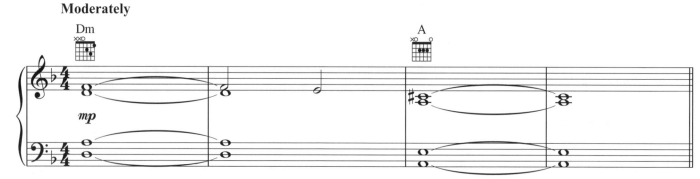

Well, you hold __ the line __ when ev-'ry one of them is giv-ing up and giv-ing in, tell me.

In this house __ of mine, __ noth-ing ev - er comes with-out a con-se-quence or cost, tell me.

PIANO / VOCAL / GUITAR

IMAGINE DRAGONS

ORIGINS

ISBN 978-1-5400-4472-3

HAL•LEONARD®

Contact us:
Hal Leonard
7777 West Bluemound Road
Milwaukee, WI 53213
Email: info@halleonard.com

In Europe, contact:
Hal Leonard Europe Limited
42 Wigmore Street
Marylebone, London, W1U 2RN
Email: info@halleonardeurope.com

In Australia, contact:
Hal Leonard Australia Pty. Ltd.
4 Lentara Court
Cheltenham, Victoria, 3192 Australia
Email: info@halleonard.com.au

Will the stars_ a - lign?_ Will heav-en step in, will it save us from our sin, will it?

'Cause this house_ of mine__ stands strong.__ That's the price you pay._

Leave be - hind your heart - ache, cast a - way._

Just an - oth - er prod - uct of to - day._

Rath - er be the hunt - er than the prey.

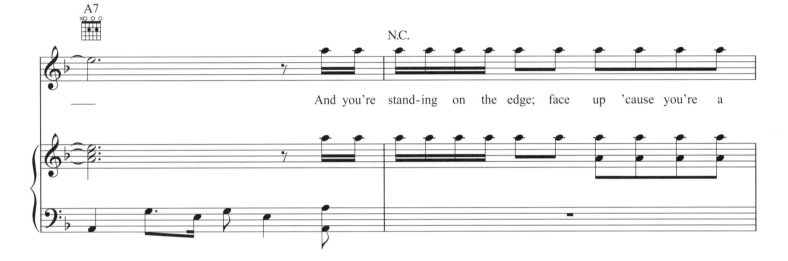

And you're stand-ing on the edge; face up 'cause you're a

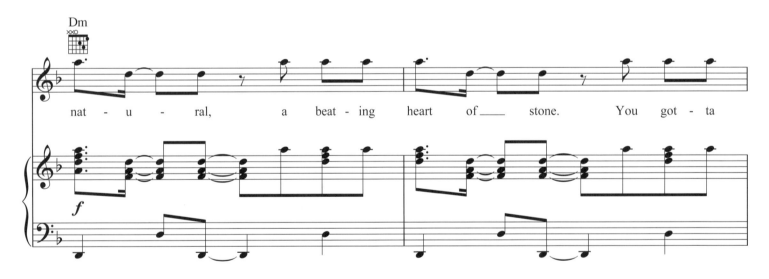

nat - u - ral, a beat-ing heart of ___ stone. You got - ta

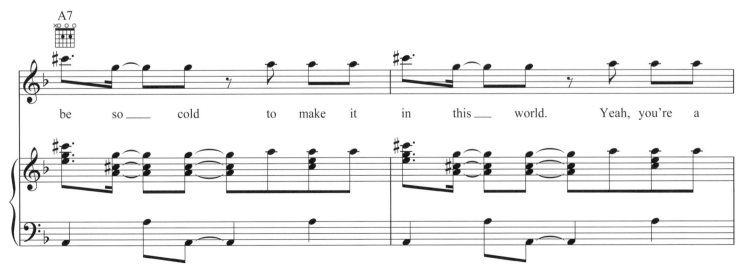

be so ___ cold to make it in this ___ world. Yeah, you're a

nat - u - ral, liv-ing your life cut-throat. You got-ta

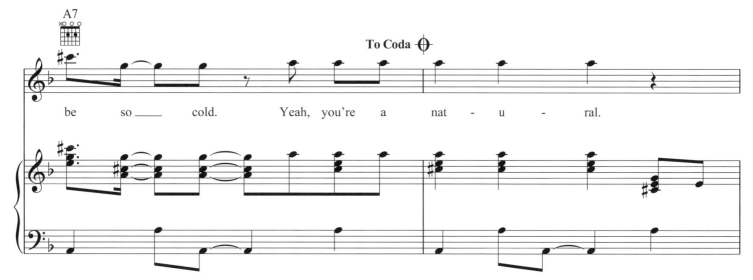

be so ___ cold. Yeah, you're a nat - u - ral.

Will some-bod-y _____ let me see the light with-in the dark trees' shad-ows and

what's hap - pen-ing? ___ Look-ing through the glass, find the wrong with-in the past, know-ing,

oh, we are __ the youth. __ Call out to the beast, not a word with-out the peace, fac-ing

D.S. al Coda

a bit of __ the truth, __ the truth. __ That's the price you pay. _

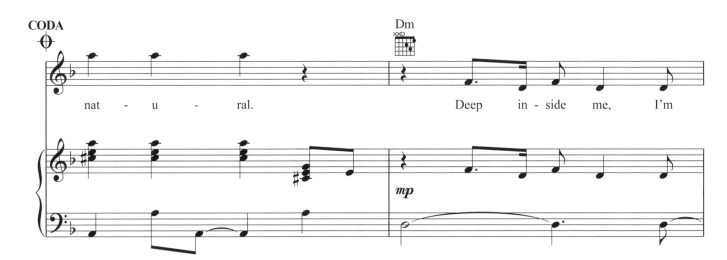

CODA

nat - u - ral. Deep in-side me, I'm

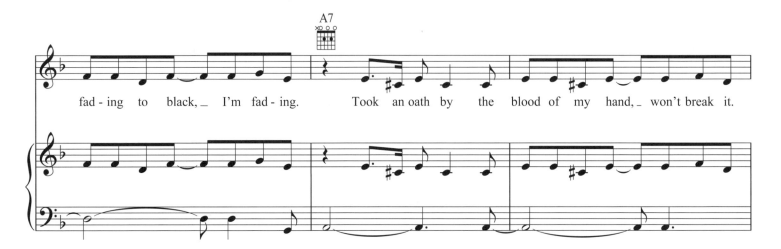

fad-ing to black, _ I'm fad-ing. Took an oath by the blood of my hand, _ won't break it.

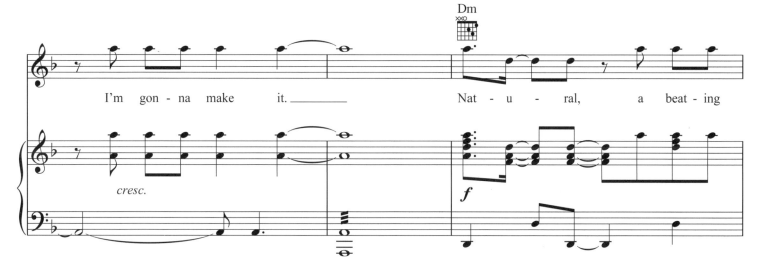

life cut - throat. You got - ta be so ___ cold. Yeah, you're a

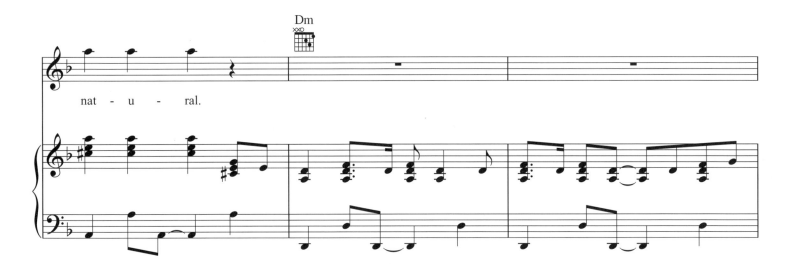

nat - u - ral.

Nat - u - ral.

Yeah, you're a nat - u - ral.

BOOMERANG

Words and Music by DAN REYNOLDS,
WAYNE SERMON, BEN McKEE,
DANIEL PLATZMAN and JORGEN ODEGARD

With movement

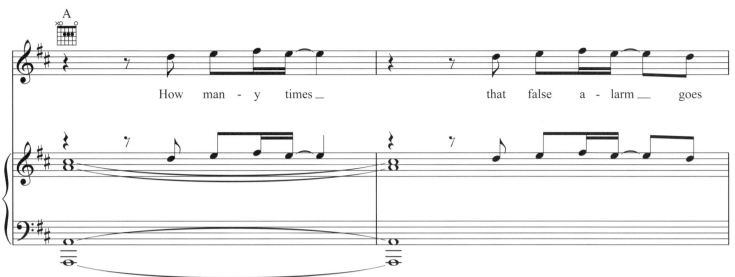

How man - y times ___ that false a - larm ___ goes

off? _____ (Goes off.) _____ Goes off. _____ (Goes off.) _____

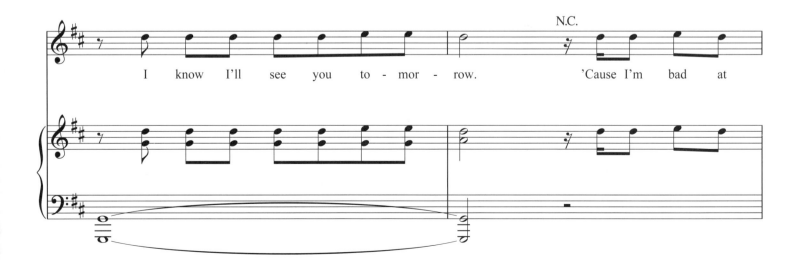

I know I'll see you to - mor - row. 'Cause I'm bad at

let - ting you go, ___ let - ting you go, let - ting you go, ___ let - ting you go.

Mov - ing on, ___ mov - ing on, mov - ing on, ___ mov - ing on. ___ I'm

read - y to go, ___ read - y to go, read - y to throw, read - y to throw.

To Coda ⊕

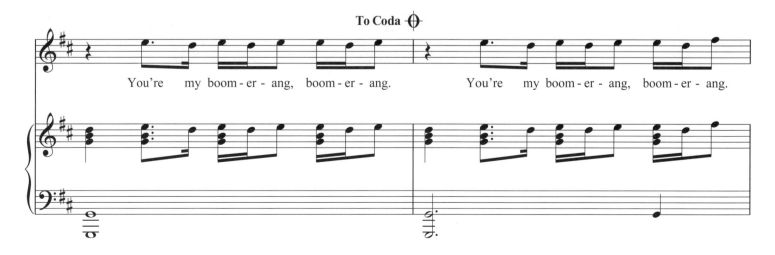

You're my boom - er - ang, boom - er - ang. You're my boom - er - ang, boom - er - ang.

CODA

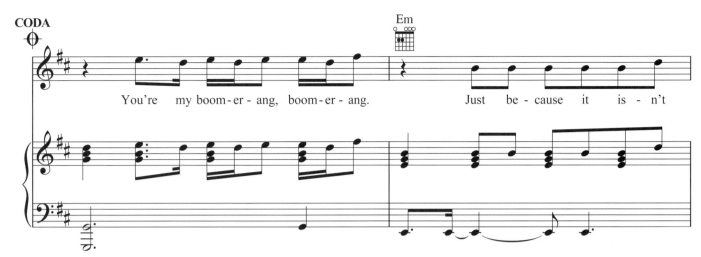

You're my boom-er - ang, boom-er - ang. Just be - cause it is - n't

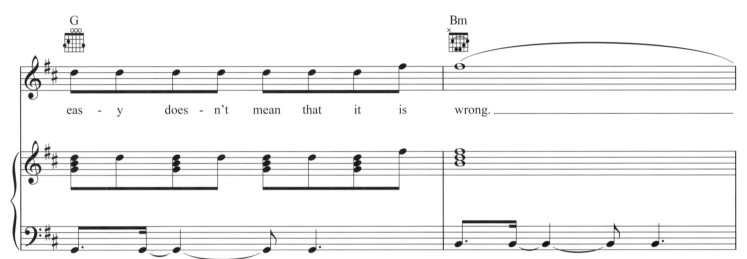

eas - y does - n't mean that it is wrong.

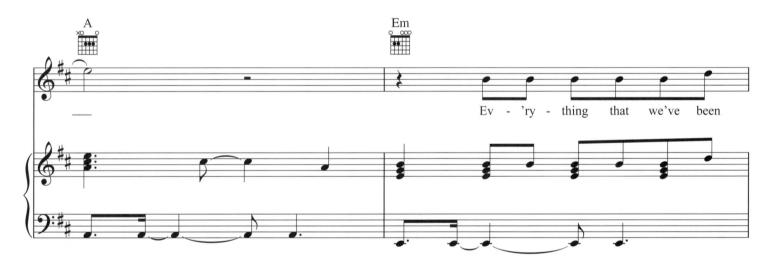

Ev - 'ry - thing that we've been

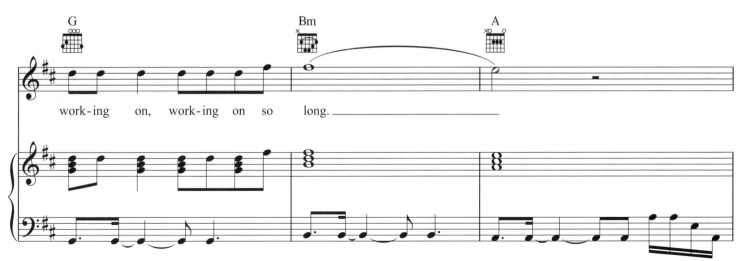

work - ing on, work - ing on so long.

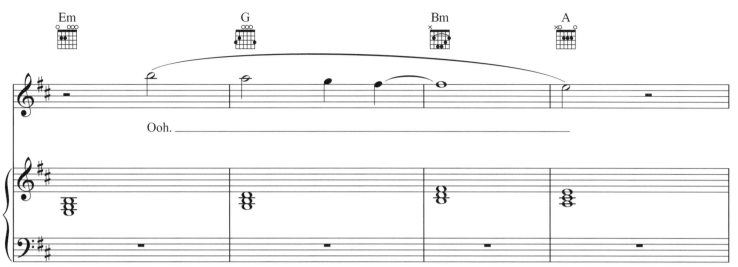

Ooh. _____

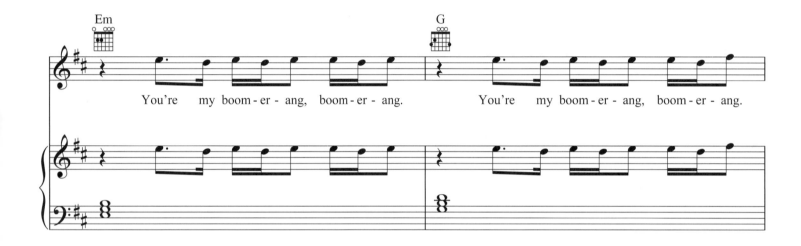

You're my boom-er-ang, boom-er-ang. You're my boom-er-ang, boom-er-ang.

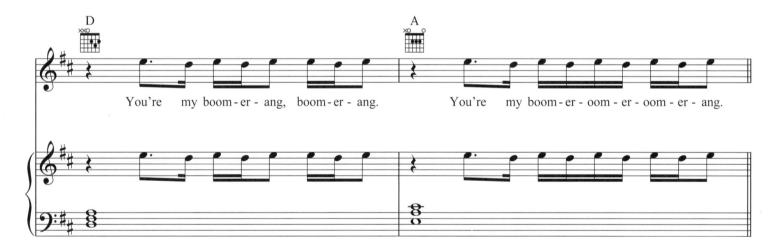

You're my boom-er-ang, boom-er-ang. You're my boom-er-oom-er-oom-er-ang.

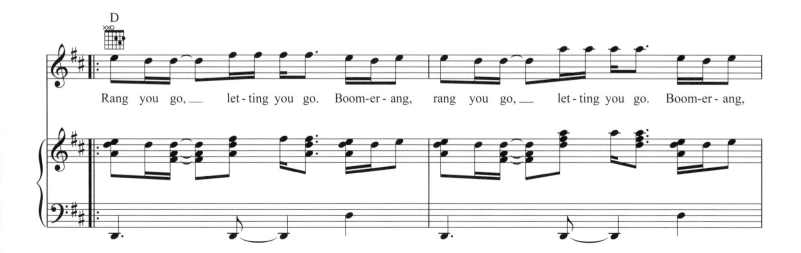

Rang you go, ___ let-ting you go. Boom-er-ang, rang you go, ___ let-ting you go. Boom-er-ang,

MACHINE

Words and Music by DAN REYNOLDS,
WAYNE SERMON, BEN McKEE,
DANIEL PLATZMAN and ALEXANDER GRANT

All my life been sit - tin' at the ta - ble, watch - in' them kids, they're liv - in' in a fa - ble.
I'm not scared of what _ you're gon-na tell me. No, I'm not scared of the beast in the bel - ly.

Looks, luck, mon - ey and nev - er left a - wish - in', but now it's 'bout time to raise _ up and pe - ti - tion.
Fill my cup with end - less am - bi - tion, and paint this town with my ver - y own vi - sion.

part of __ your ma - chine. __

I am the ma-chine.

'Cause I've been won-der-in'
I am the ma-chine.

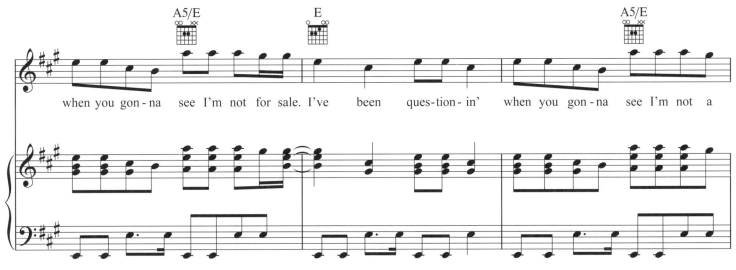

when you gon - na see I'm not for sale. I've been ques-tion-in' when you gon - na see I'm not a

part of ___ your ma - chine, ___   not a part of ___ your ma - chine. ___

'Cause ___   I am the ma - chine. ___

COOL OUT

Words and Music by DAN REYNOLDS,
WAYNE SERMON, BEN McKEE,
DANIEL PLATZMAN and TIM RANDOLPH

With a groove

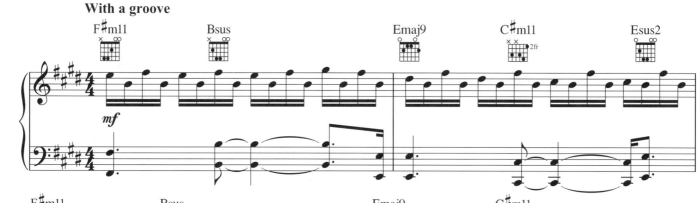

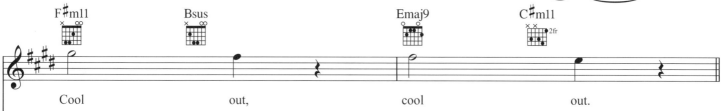

Cool out, cool out.

Just be-fore __ I go, __ yes, I know that I'm los-ing con-trol __ and

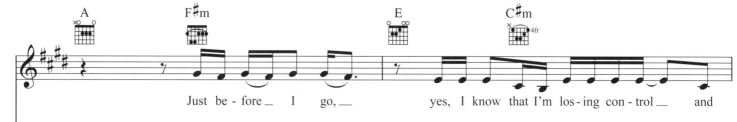

I want to take things slow, put my mind in cruise con-trol. _____

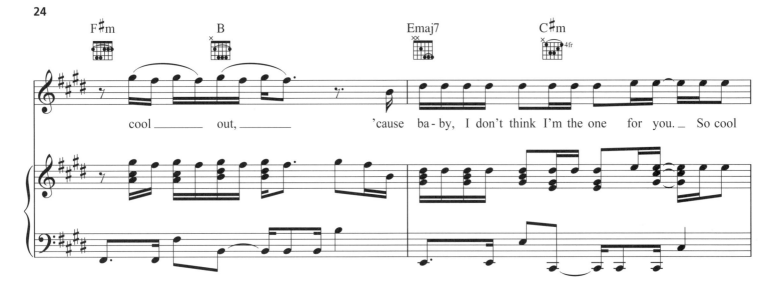

cool _____ out, _____ 'cause ba-by, I don't think I'm the one for you. _ So cool

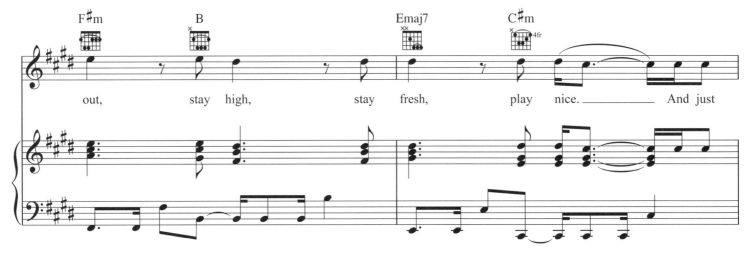

out, stay high, stay fresh, play nice. _____ And just

To Coda

cool _____ out _____ 'cause ba-by, I don't think I'm the one for you. _ So cool

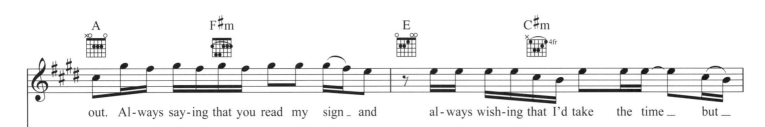

out. Al-ways say-ing that you read my sign _ and al-ways wish-ing that I'd take the time _ but _

25

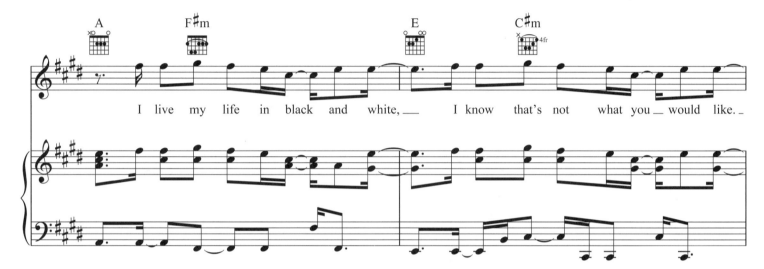

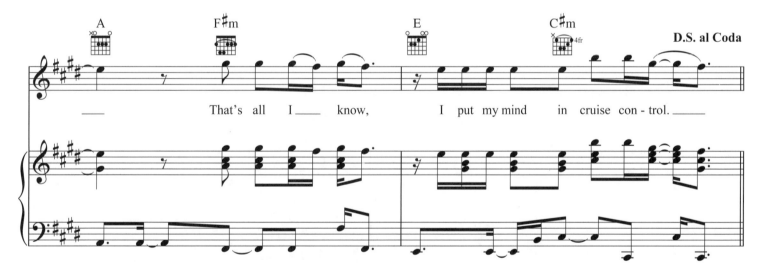

ba-by, I don't think I'm the one for you.__ So cool out, stay high, stay

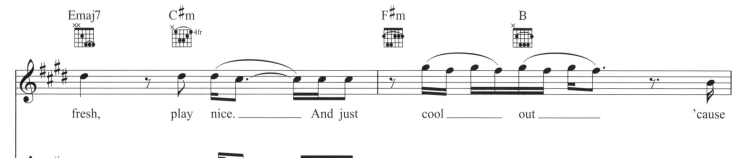

fresh, play nice._____ And just cool_____ out_____ 'cause

Cool out, so cool

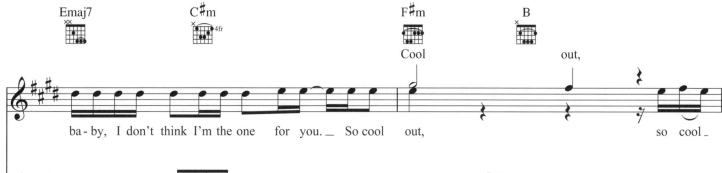

ba-by, I don't think I'm the one for you.__ So cool out, so cool__

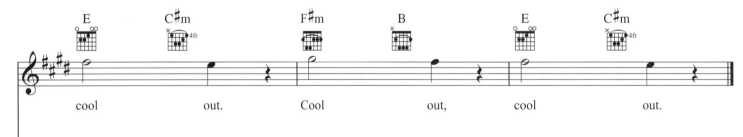

BAD LIAR

Words and Music by DAN REYNOLDS,
WAYNE SERMON, BEN McKEE,
DANIEL PLATZMAN, JORGEN ODEGARD
and AJA VOLKMAN

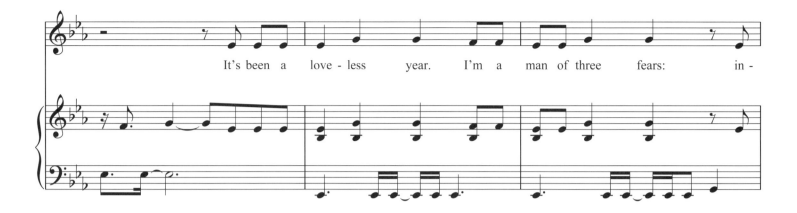

It's been a love-less year. I'm a man of three fears: in-

teg-ri-ty, faith and croc-o-dile tears. Trust me, dar-ling.

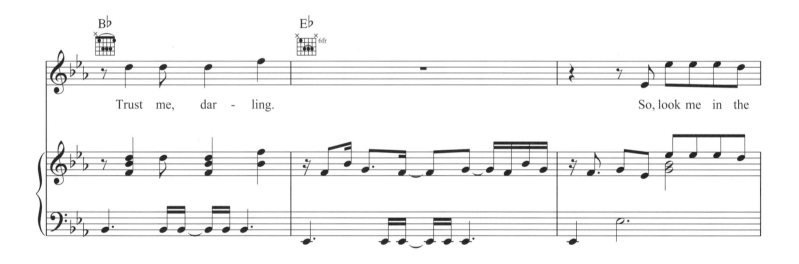

Trust me, dar-ling. So, look me in the

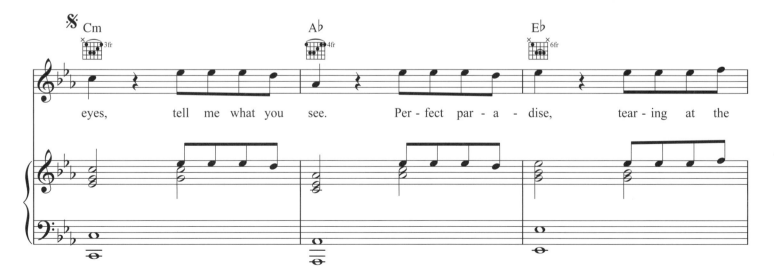

eyes, tell me what you see. Per-fect par-a-dise, tear-ing at the

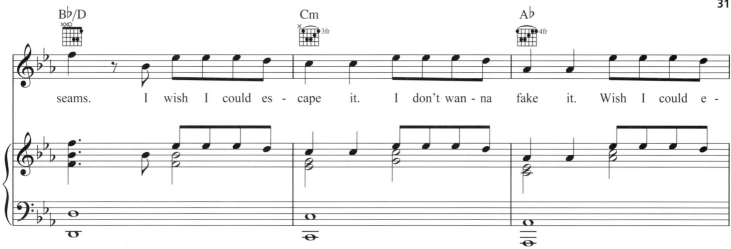

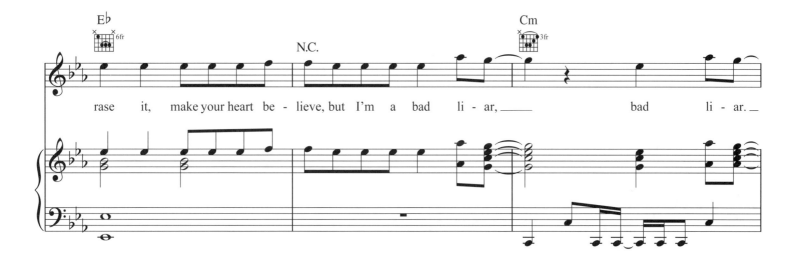

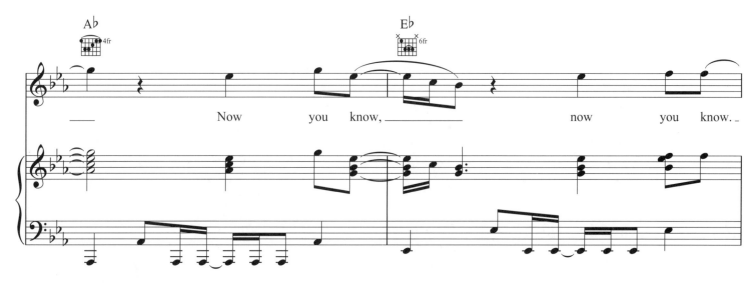

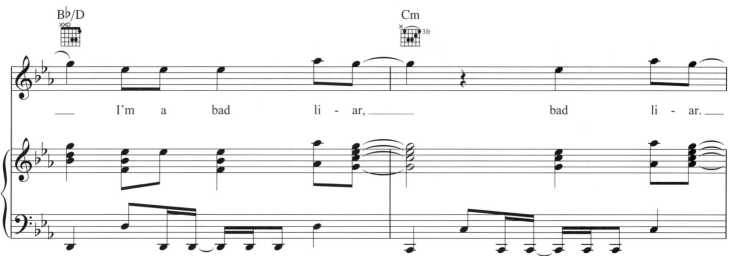

Now you know, _____ you're free to go. _____

Did all my dreams nev-er mean one thing? _ Does

hap-pi-ness lie in a dia-mond ring? _ Oh, _____ I've been ask-ing for, oh, _

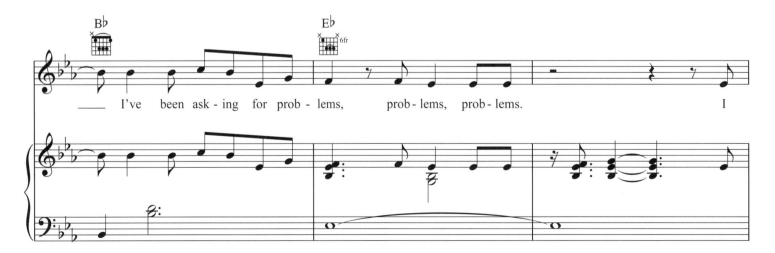

_____ I've been ask-ing for prob-lems, prob-lems, prob-lems. I

wage my war on the world in - side._____ I

take my gun to the en - e - my's side._____ Oh,___

___ I've been ask - ing for, oh,_____ I've been ask - ing for prob -

D.S. al Coda

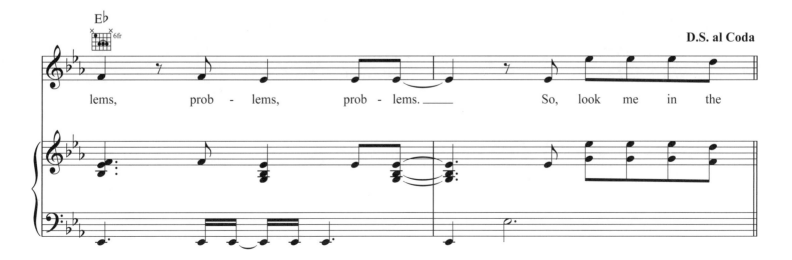

lems, prob - lems, prob - lems.____ So, look me in the

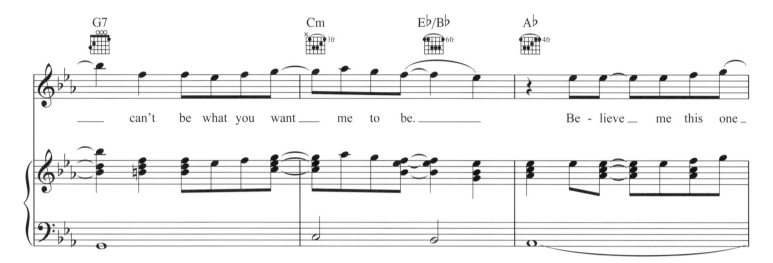

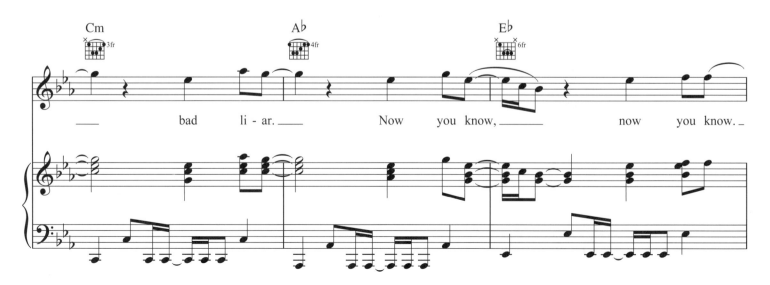

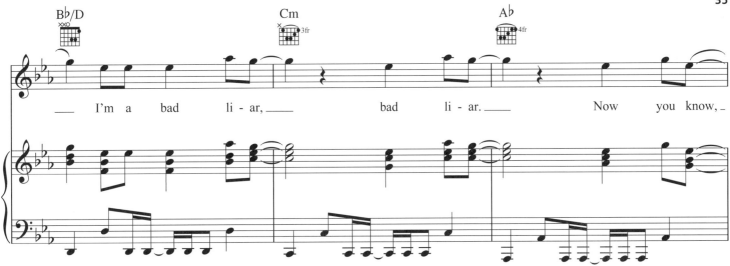

I'm a bad li-ar, _____ bad li-ar. _____ Now you know, _

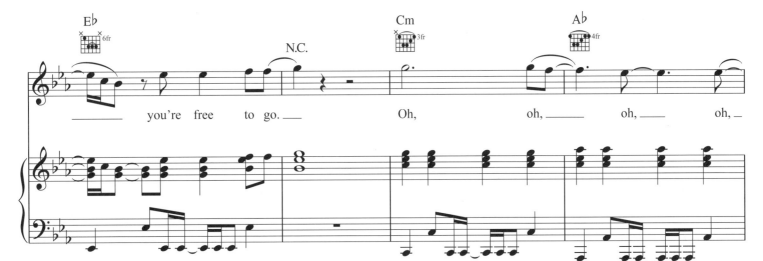

_____ you're free to go. _____ Oh, _____ oh, _____ oh, _____ oh, _

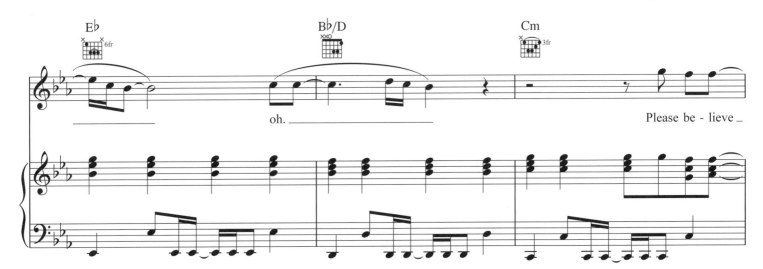

oh. _____ Please be - lieve _

_____ me, please be - lieve _____ me. _____

WEST COAST

Words and Music by DAN REYNOLDS,
WAYNE SERMON, BEN McKEE
and DANIEL PLATZMAN

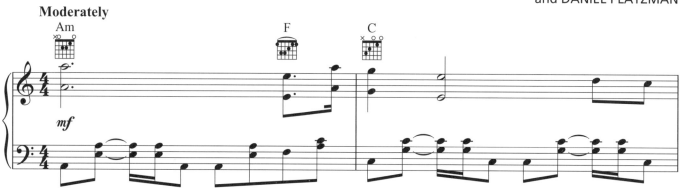

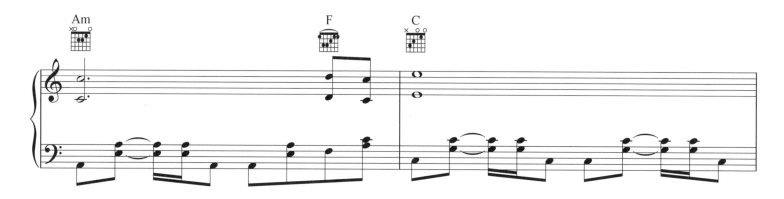

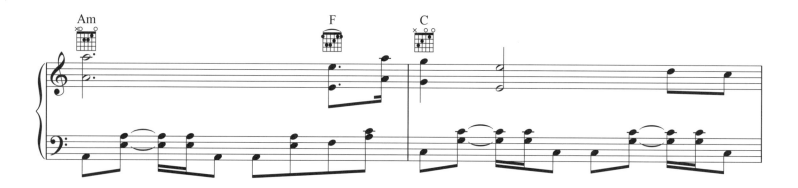

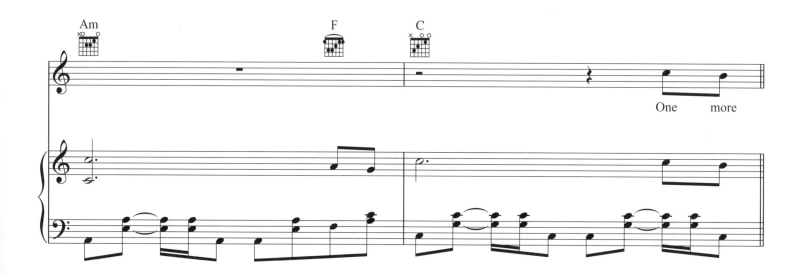

One more

day _____ we'll spend to - geth - er. _____ Lay your

eyes, look up up - on me for the bet - ter. _____ Oh, I

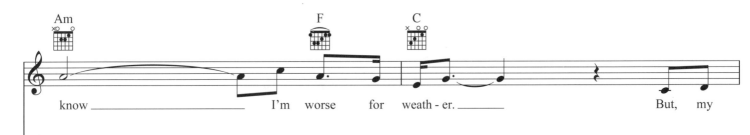

know _____ I'm worse for weath - er. _____ But, my

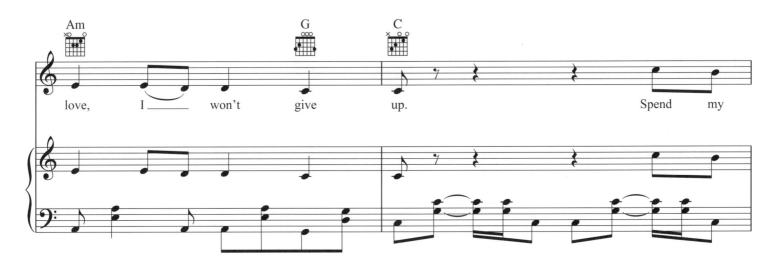

love, I _____ won't give up. Spend my

38

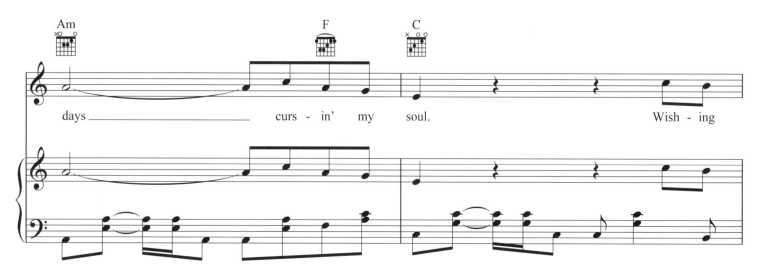

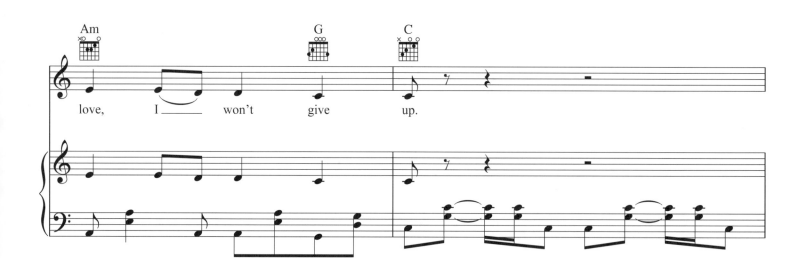

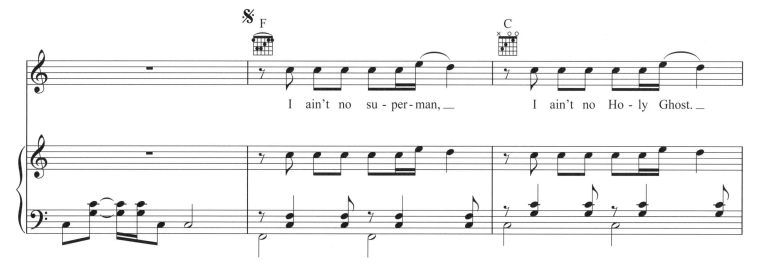

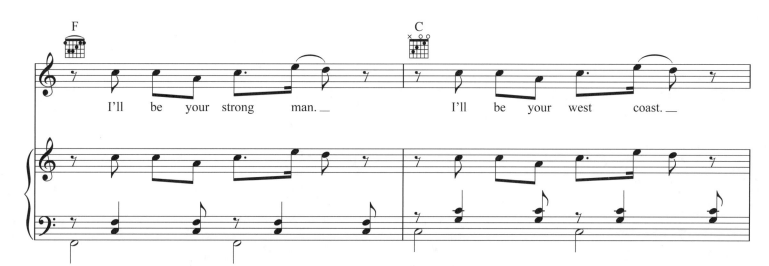

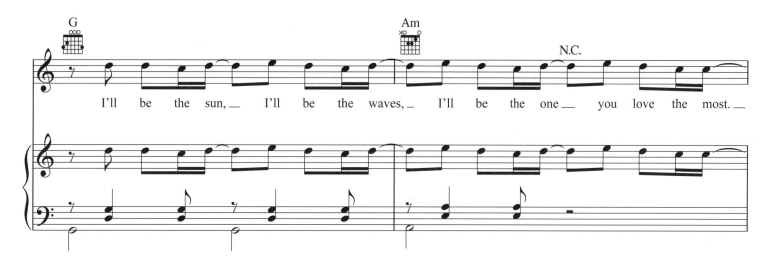

40

ooh,

ooh.

I'll change my ways _____ if you would stay. __

And all your tears that you have cried would go a-

42

way. Oh, just grant _____ me one more

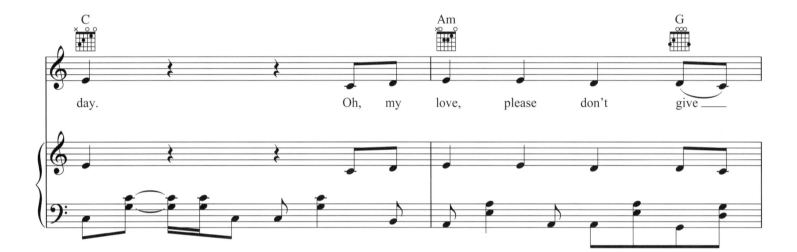

day. Oh, my love, please don't give ____

up. See the dev - il at my

door. I see the fu - ture of the ones that I've ig -

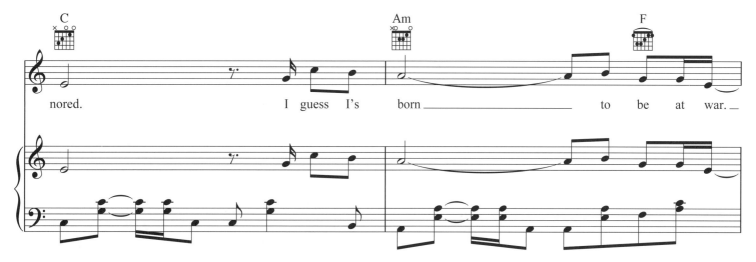

nored. I guess I's born _____ to be at war. _____

_____ And, my love, I won't give up.

So, my love, please don't give

D.S. al Coda

up.

CODA

west coast, hon-ey. Hey, hey, hey, oh, _____

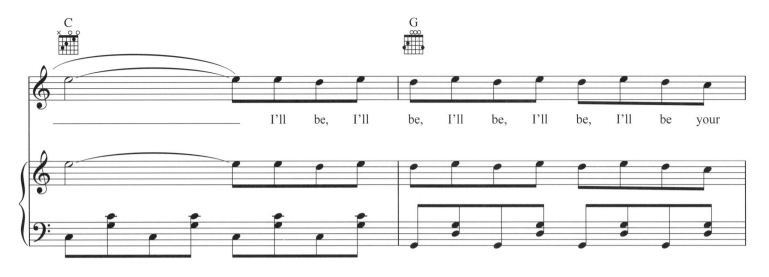

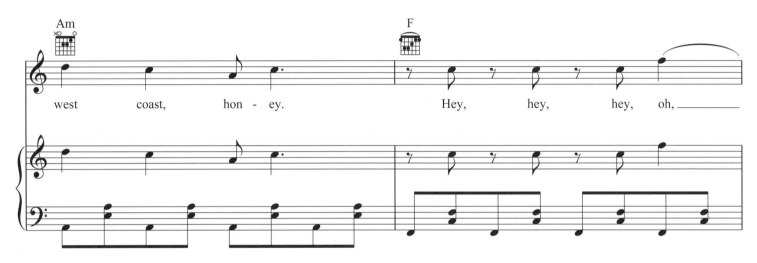

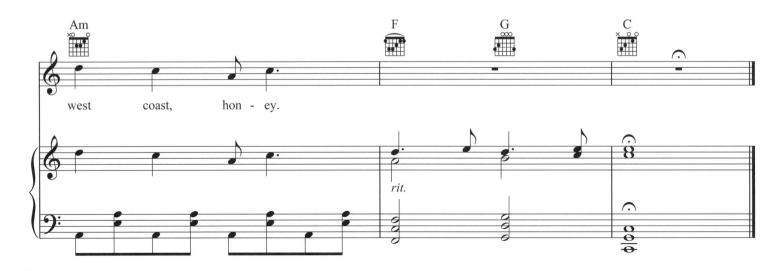

BULLET IN A GUN

Words and Music by DAN REYNOLDS,
WAYNE SERMON, BEN McKEE, DANIEL PLATZMAN,
JAYSON DeZUZIO and ALEXANDER GRANT

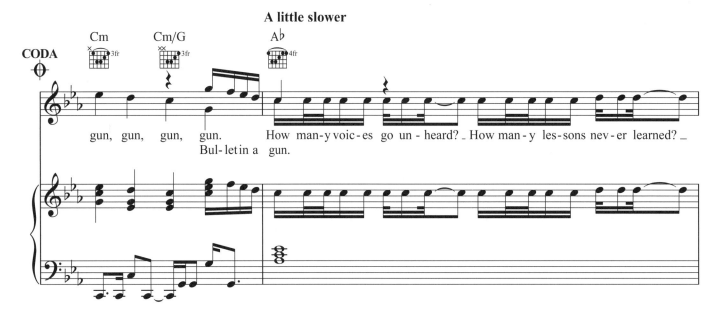

gun, gun, gun, gun. How man-y voic-es go un - heard? How man-y les-sons nev-er learned?
Bul-let in a gun.

How man-y ar-tists fear the light? Fear the pain, go in - sane?

Lose your mind, lose your-self, you on - ly care a - bout fame and wealth.

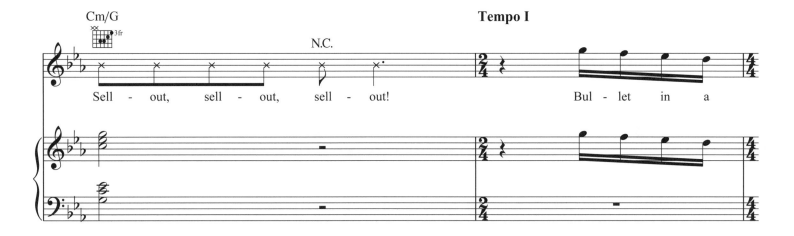

Sell - out, sell - out, sell - out! Bul - let in a

ZERO
from RALPH BREAKS THE INTERNET

Words and Music by DAN REYNOLDS,
WAYNE SERMON, BEN McKEE,
DANIEL PLATZMAN and JOHN HILL

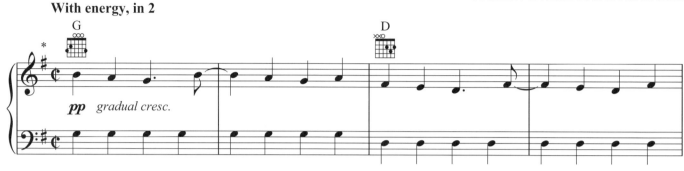

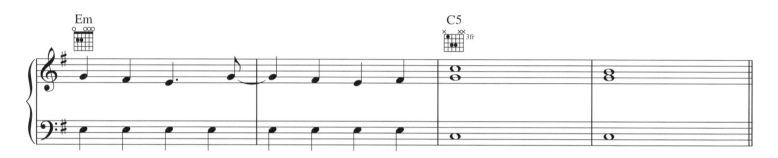

I find it hard to say the things I wan-na say the most, find a lit-tle bit of
I find it hard to tell you how I wan-na run a-way. I un-der-stand it al-ways

stead-y as I get close, find a bal-ance in the mid-dle of the cha-os.
makes you feel a cer-tain way. I find a bal-ance in the mid-dle of the cha-os.

* *Recorded a half step lower.*

51

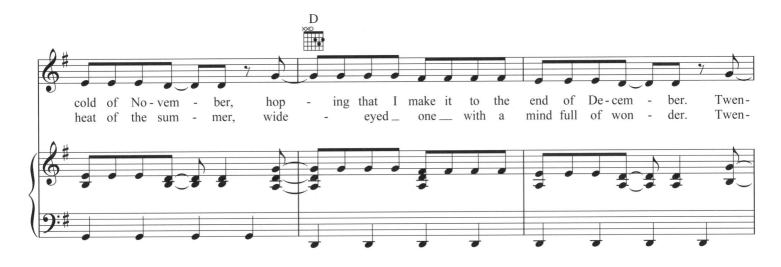

- -ing for the path of the young and lone - ly. I _____ don't wan - na hear a - bout
- -ing for the path of the young and lone - ly. I _____ don't wan - na hear a - bout

what to do. _____ I _____ don't wan - na do it just to do it for you. _____
what to do, _____ no. I _____ don't wan - na do it just to do it for you. _____

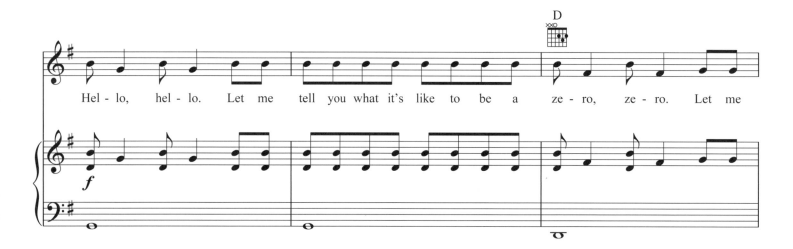

Hel - lo, hel - lo. Let me tell you what it's like to be a ze - ro, ze - ro. Let me

show you what it's like to al - ways feel, _____ feel _____ like I'm emp - ty and there's noth - ing real - ly

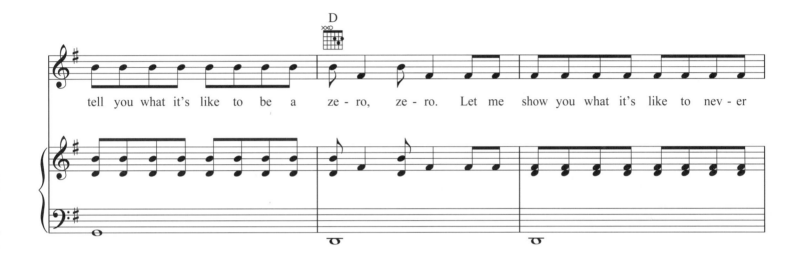

A little slower, with some freedom

Let me tell you 'bout it, let me tell you 'bout it. May-be you're the same as me.

Let me tell you 'bout it, let me tell you 'bout it. They say the truth will set you free.

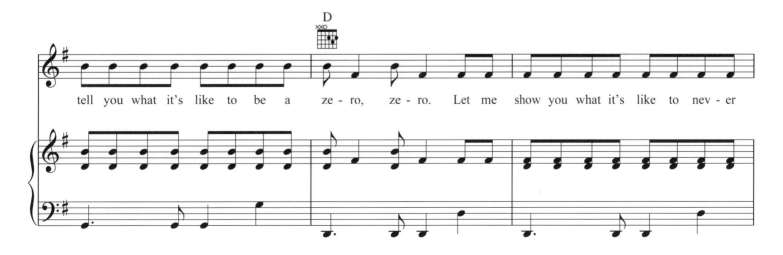

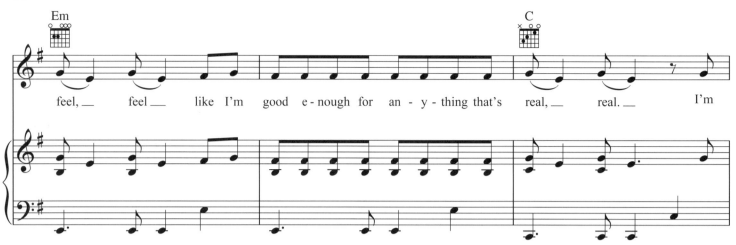

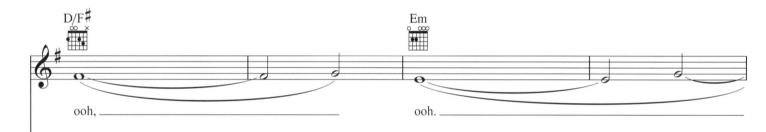

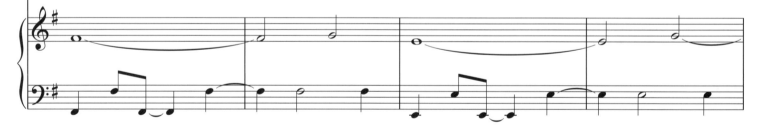

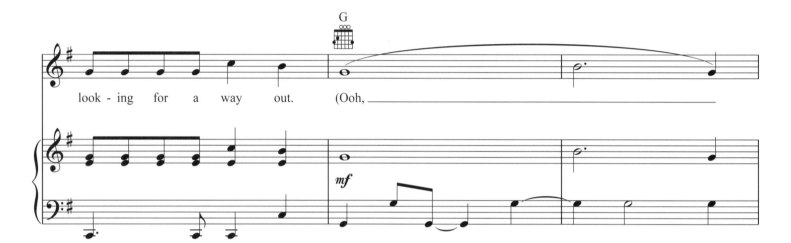

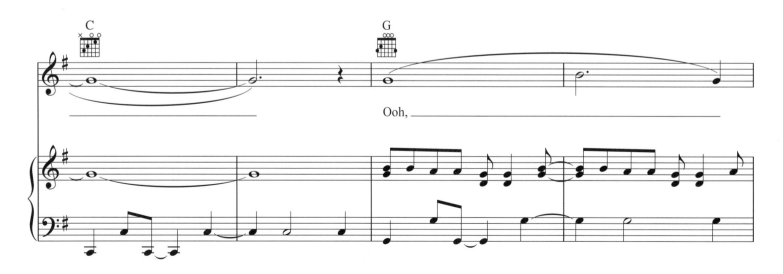

ooh, _____ ooh.) _____

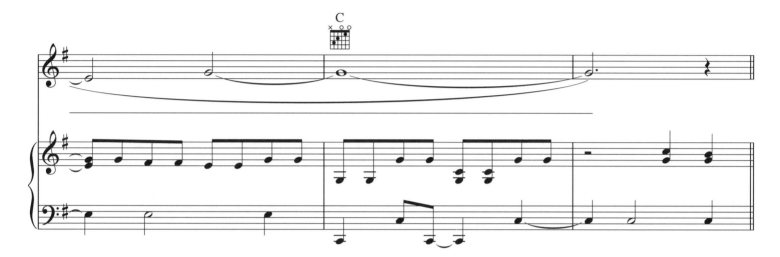

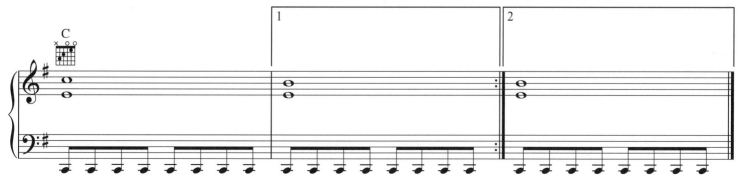

DIGITAL

Words and Music by DAN REYNOLDS,
WAYNE SERMON, BEN McKEE,
DANIEL PLATZMAN and ALEXANDER GRANT

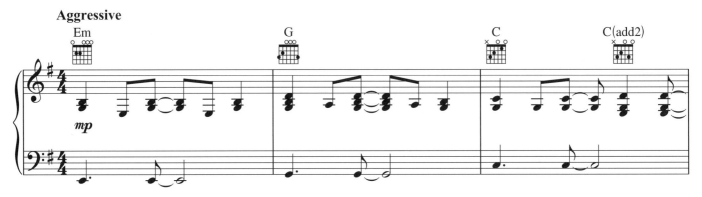

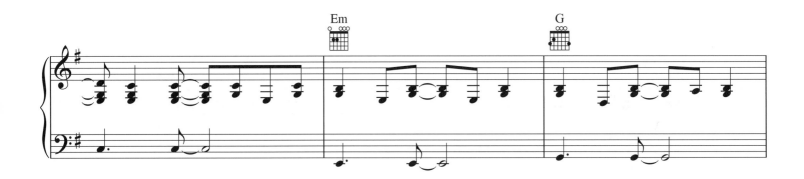

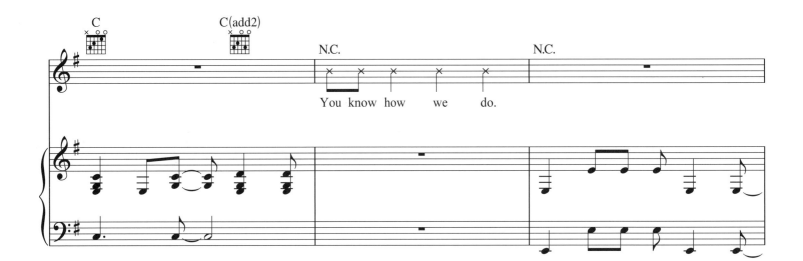

You know how we do.

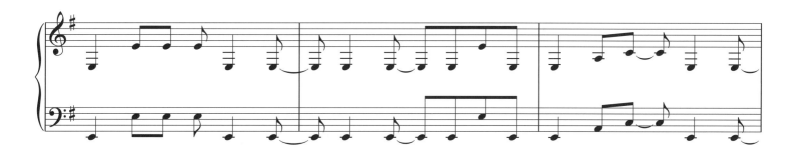

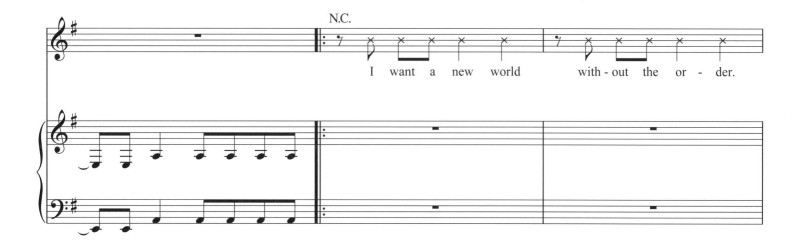

I want a new world with-out the or - der.

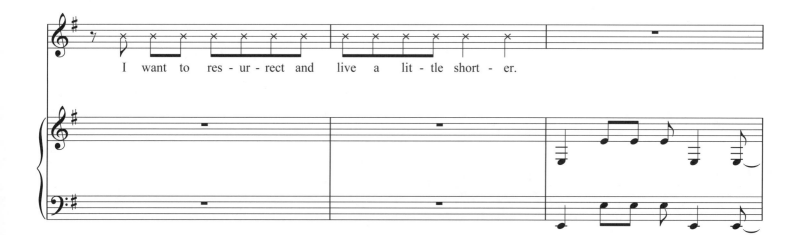

I want to res - ur - rect and live a lit - tle short - er.

I want it heav - y, I want the fu - ry, I want to beat out the

judge and the ju - ry.

Em

From the out - side, _

_ ev - 'ry - thing _ looks right. _ From the out - side, _ from the out - side.

D/E

C/E

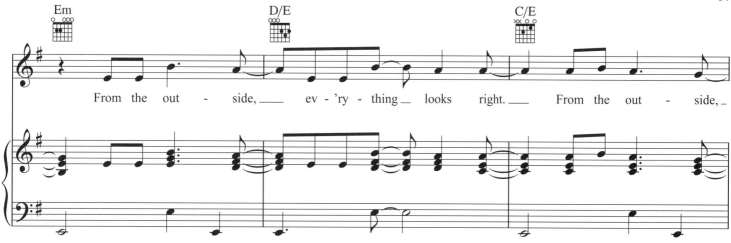

From the out - side, ___ ev - 'ry - thing ___ looks right. ___ From the out - side, _

___ from the out - side. We are, ___ we are the face of the fu - ture.

We are, ___ we are the dig - i - tal heart - beat. We are, ___ we are the

face of the fu - ture. We don't want to change, we just want to change ev - 'ry - thing!

Ay, ay, ay, ay, dig-i-tal, dig-i-tal. Ay, ay, ay, ay,

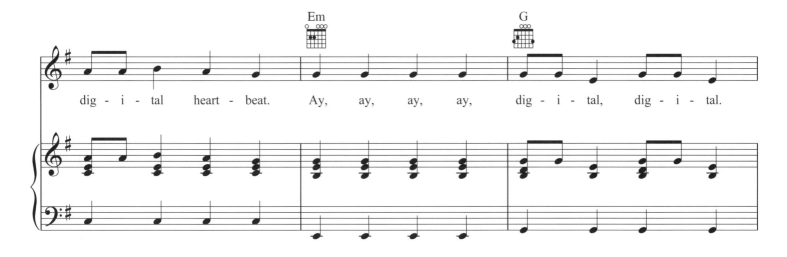

dig-i-tal heart-beat. Ay, ay, ay, ay, dig-i-tal, dig-i-tal.

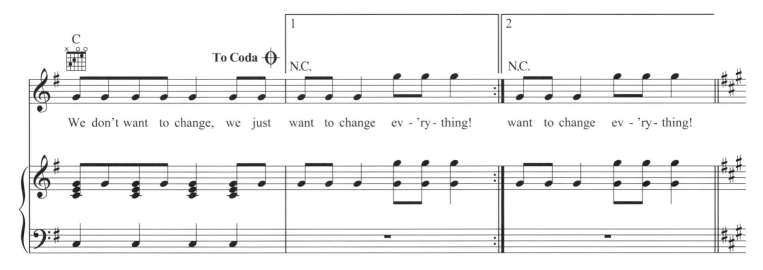

We don't want to change, we just want to change ev-'ry-thing! want to change ev-'ry-thing!

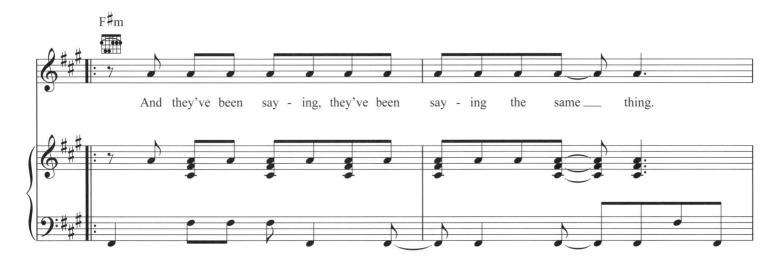

And they've been say-ing, they've been say-ing the same ___ thing.

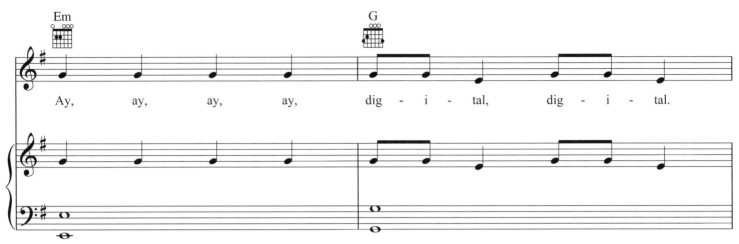

Ay, ay, ay, ay, dig - i - tal, dig - i - tal.

Ay, ay, ay, ay, dig - i - tal heart - beat.

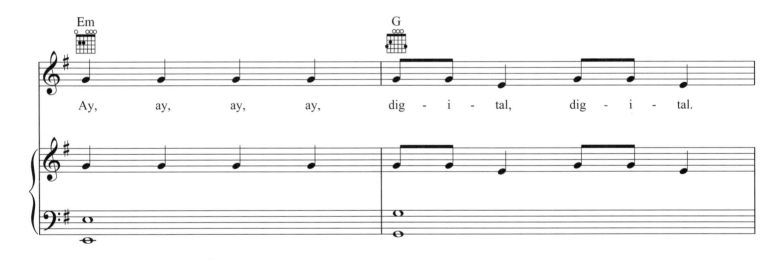

Ay, ay, ay, ay, dig - i - tal, dig - i - tal.

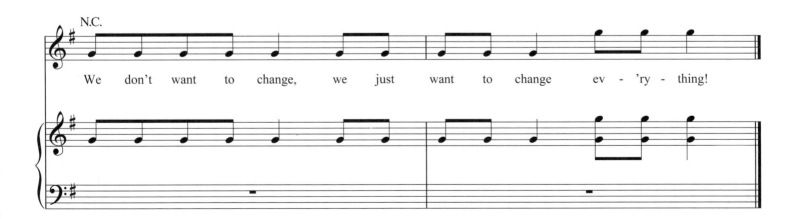

We don't want to change, we just want to change ev - 'ry - thing!

ONLY

Words and Music by DAN REYNOLDS,
WAYNE SERMON, BEN McKEE,
DANIEL PLATZMAN, ROBIN FREDRIKSSON,
MATTIAS LARSSON and JUSTIN TRANTER

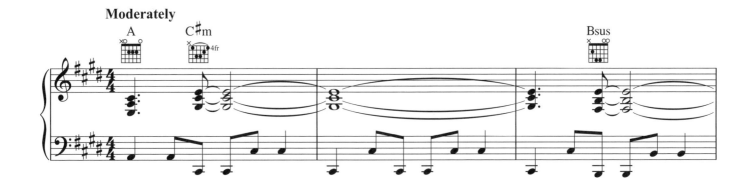

Oh, pret-ty ba - by, you're ___ my mot-i-vat - or.
My dis-as - ter, you're ___ my on-ly an - swer.

Got me chang-in' my words ___ and my be-hav - ior.
You got me think-in' that I ___ could be your mas - ter.

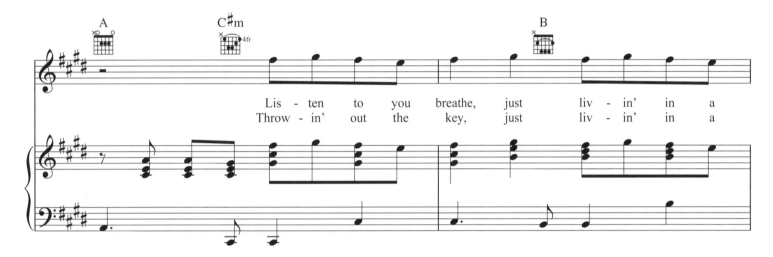

STUCK

Words and Music by DAN REYNOLDS,
WAYNE SERMON, BEN McKEE,
DANIEL PLATZMAN, JAYSON DeZUZIO,
ALEXANDER GRANT and AJA VOLKMAN

Moderately

Time goes by ___ and still ___ I'm ___ stuck on you. ___

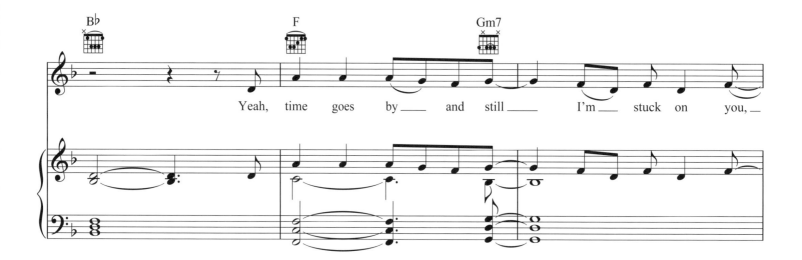

Yeah, time goes by ___ and still ___ I'm ___ stuck on you, ___

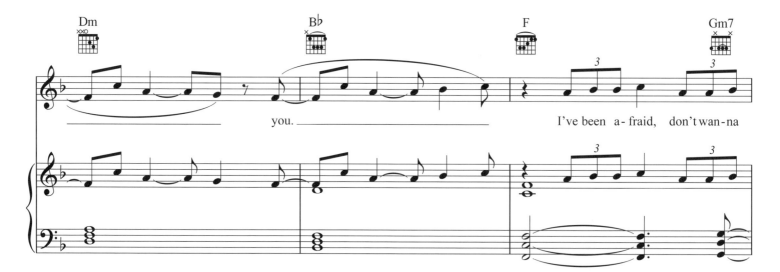

you. ___ I've been a-fraid, don't wan-na

fade out of my bod - y. ___ I've been a-stray, bare-ly a - wake, float-ing a-bove me. ___

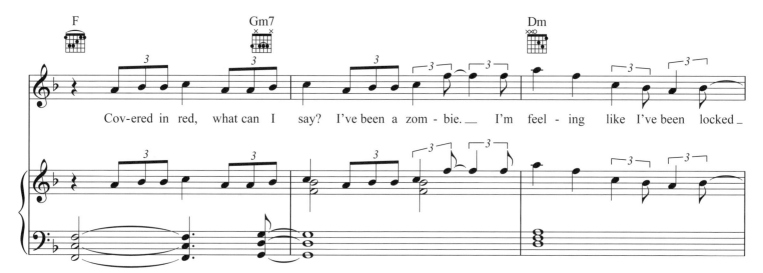

Cov-ered in red, what can I say? I've been a zom - bie. ___ I'm feel - ing like I've been locked ___

___ in a grave. _ You were the laugh, you were the life, you were the par - ty. ___

You were the brave, I was the weak, you were the ar - my. ___ You were the faith, you were the

truth, I was the sor - ry.___ I'm feel - ing like you've been tak - en a - way. You were my

one, you were my one. When all has been said, all has been

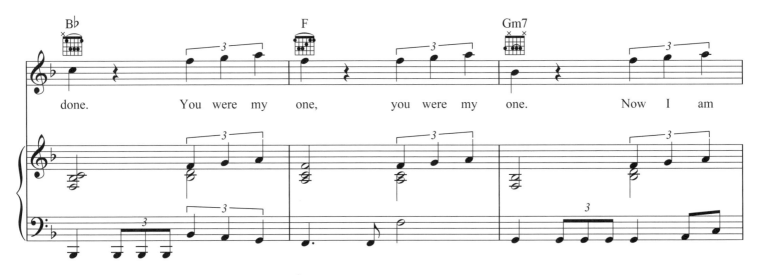

done. You were my one, you were my one. Now I am

left reach - ing a - bove me, oh, oh. Time goes by ___ and still ___

I'm _____ stuck on you, _____ you. _____

Time goes by ___ and still ___ I'm ___ stuck on you, _____ you. ___

To Coda ⊕

_____ Why did you leave? Why did you go leav-ing me lone - ly? ___

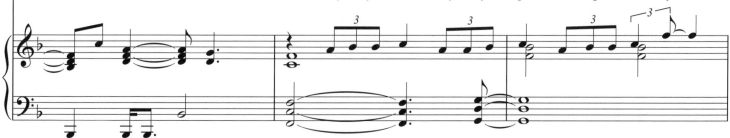

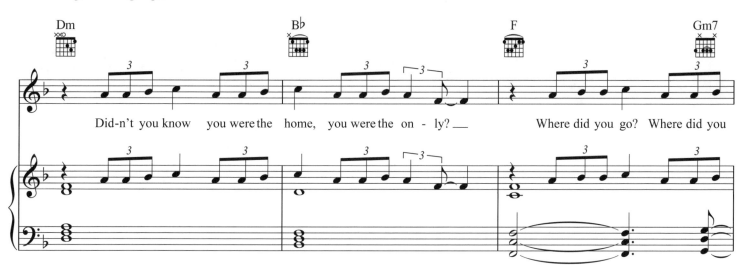

Did-n't you know you were the home, you were the on - ly? ___ Where did you go? Where did you

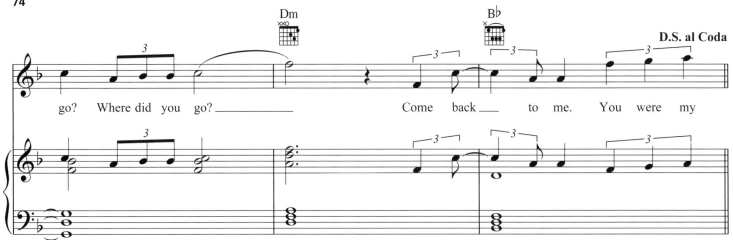

go? Where did you go? _____ Come back ___ to me. You were my

Time goes by ___ and still ___ I'm ___ stuck on you. ___

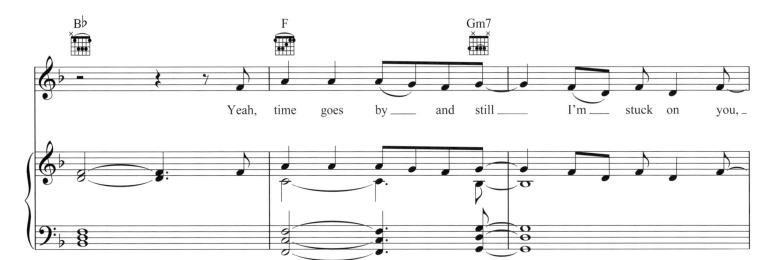

Yeah, time goes by ___ and still ___ I'm ___ stuck on you, _

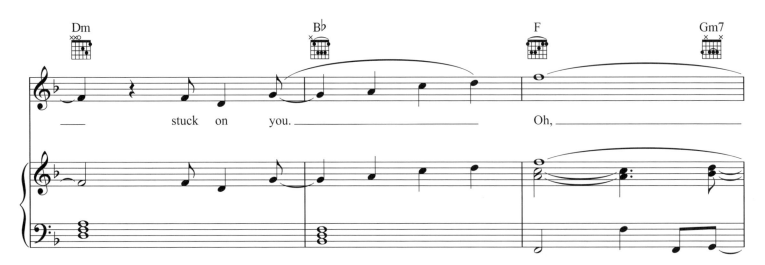

___ stuck on you. _____ Oh, _____

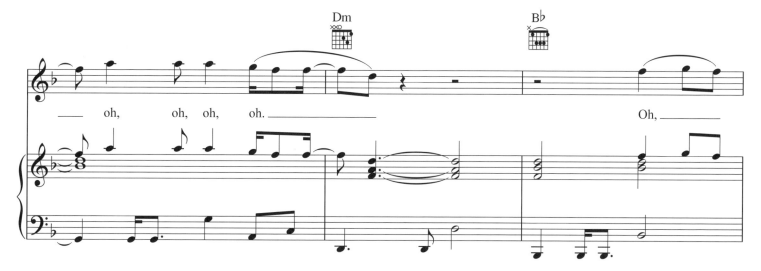

oh,   oh,   oh,   oh.   Oh, _____

oh, _____ oh,   oh,   oh,   oh. _____

Whoa,   oh. _____ Time goes by ___ and still ___ I'm ___ stuck on you, ___

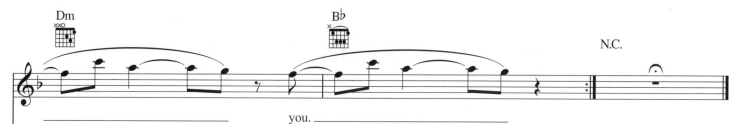

you. _____

LOVE

Words and Music by DAN REYNOLDS,
WAYNE SERMON, BEN McKEE,
DANIEL PLATZMAN and IDO ZMISHLANY

talk - in' all a - bout the prob - lems, shock - in' shock - in'. We put on our

head - phones, walk - in', walk - in'. We put on our head - phones.

Where did we all ___ go wrong? ___ Love, love, love, lo, lo, lo.

Love, love, love, lo, lo, lo. Love, love,

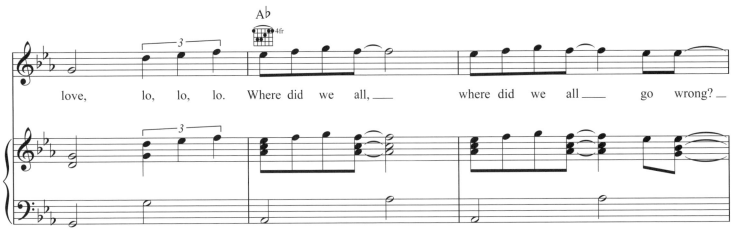

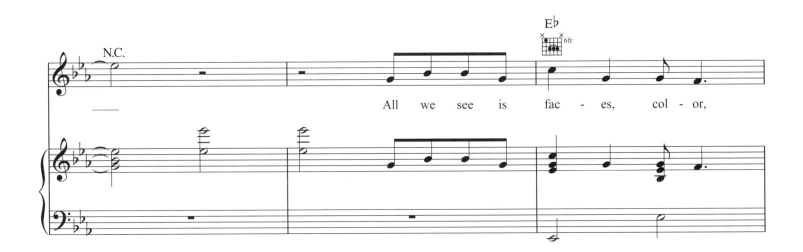

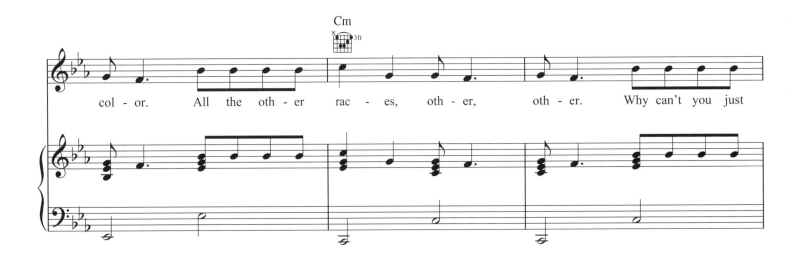

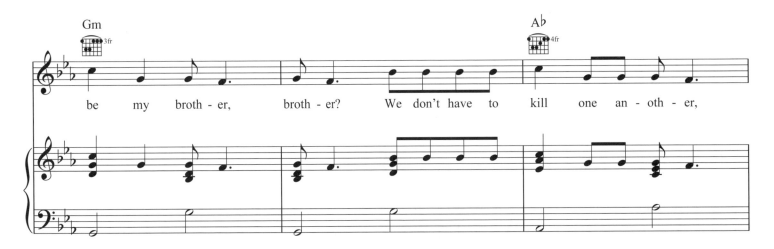

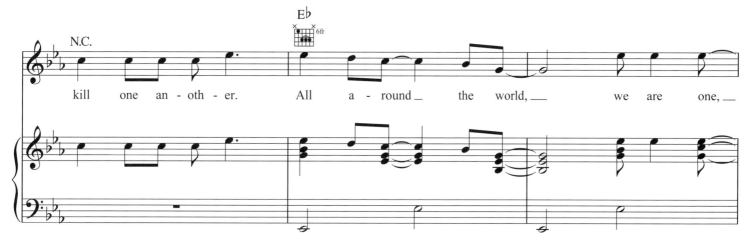

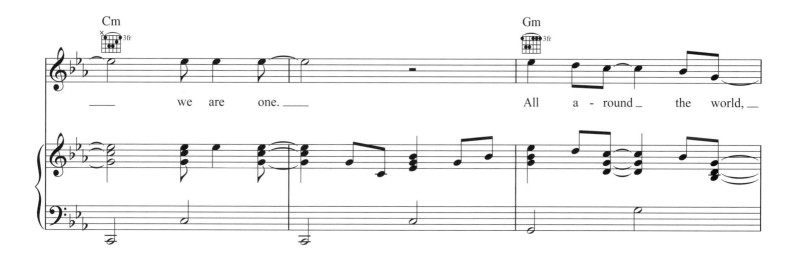

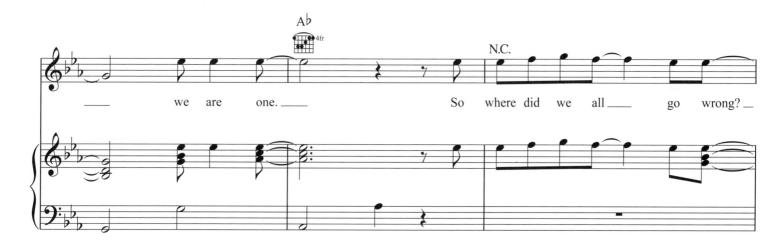

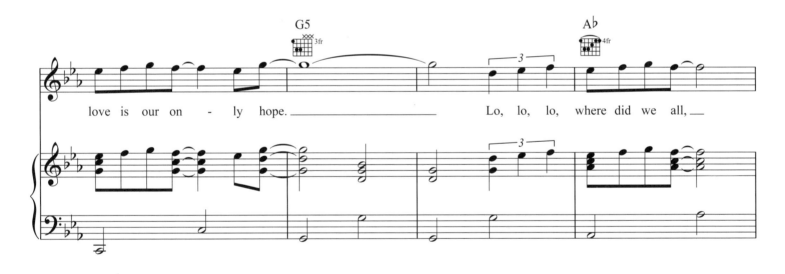

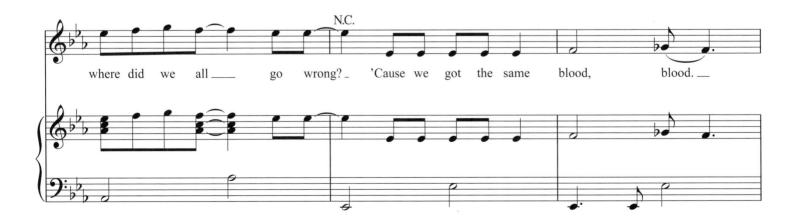

We got the same blood, _ blood. _____ But will it be e-

nough, _ nough? _ Will it be e-nough? _____

We got the same heart - beat. _ We're liv-in' for the

same _ dream. _ We got the same blood - stream. _ Where did we all go wrong? _

(Lead vocal ad lib.)

Where did we all, ___

where did we all ___ go wrong? ___ Love, love, it's dark-est be-fore ___ the dawn.

Love, love, love is our on - ly hope. ___

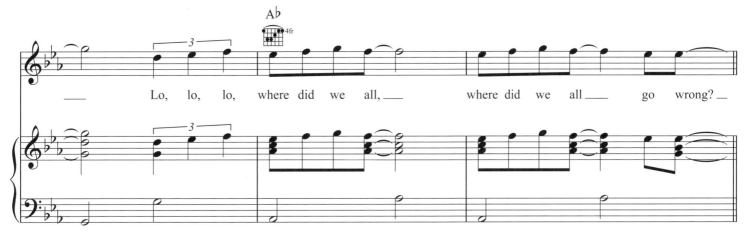

Lo, lo, lo, where did we all, ___ where did we all ___ go wrong? ___

___ Where did we all, where did we all? _____ Where did we all,
(Lead vocal ad lib.)

where did we all? _____ Where did we all, where did we all? ___

Where did we all, ___ where did we all ___ go wrong? ___

BIRDS

Words and Music by DAN REYNOLDS,
WAYNE SERMON, BEN McKEE,
DANIEL PLATZMAN and JOEL LITTLE

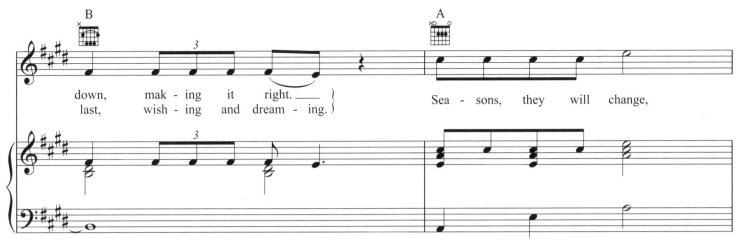

down, mak - ing it right. ___
last, wish - ing and dream - ing.
Sea - sons, they will change,

life will make you grow. Dreams will make you cry, cry, cry.

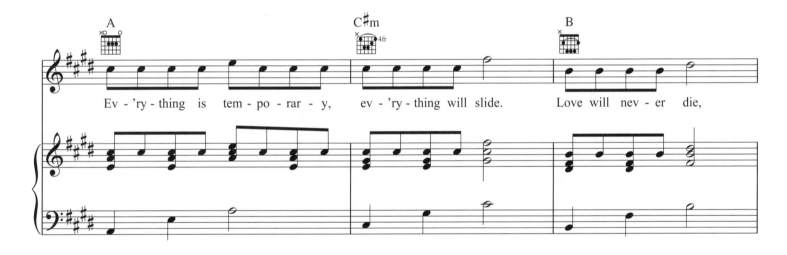

Ev - 'ry - thing is tem - po - rar - y, ev - 'ry - thing will slide. Love will nev - er die,

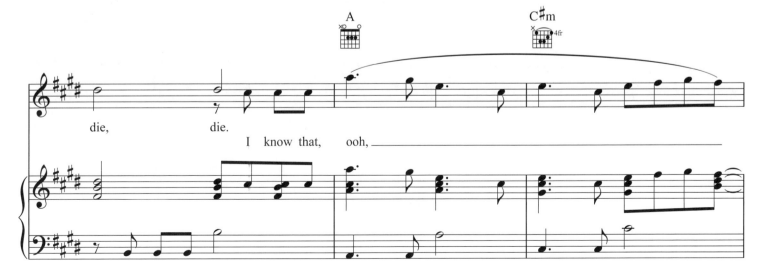

die, die. I know that, ooh, ___

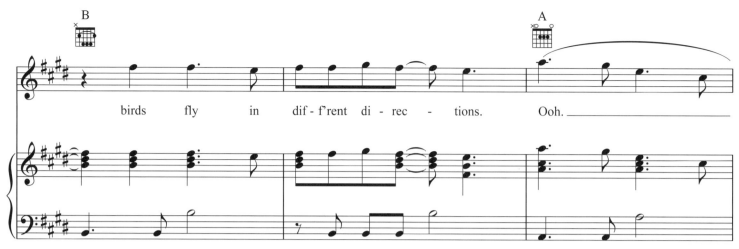

birds fly in dif-f'rent di - rec - tions. Ooh. _____

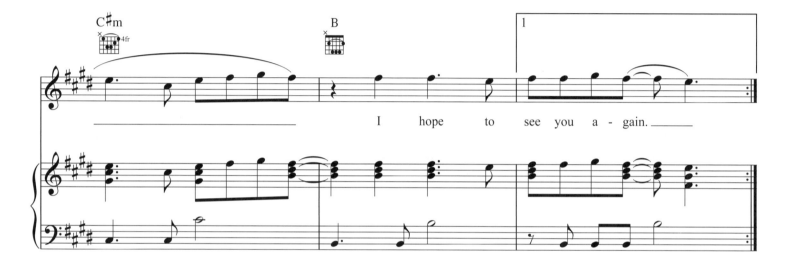

I hope to see you a - gain. _____

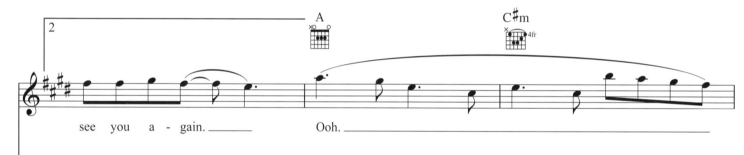

see you a - gain. _____ Ooh. _____

Birds fly in dif-f'rent di - rec - tions. Ooh. _____

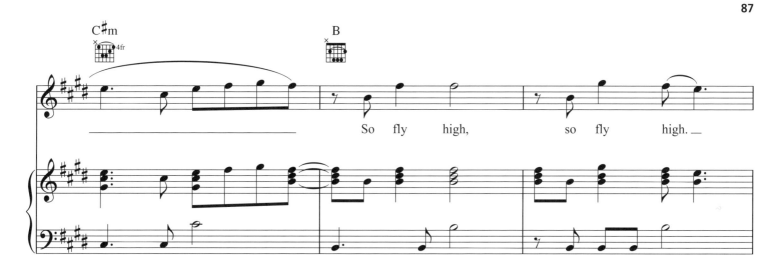

So fly high, so fly high.

When the moon is look-ing down,

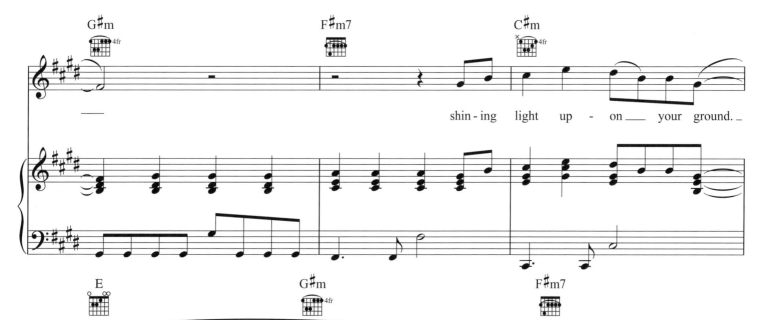

shin-ing light up-on___ your ground.

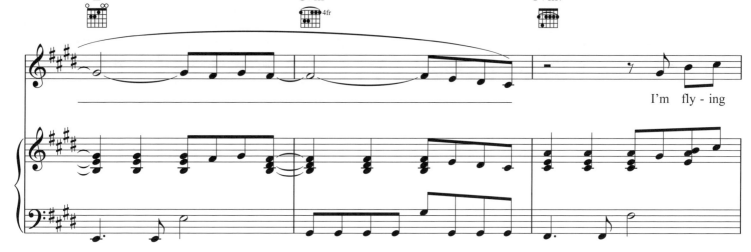

I'm fly-ing

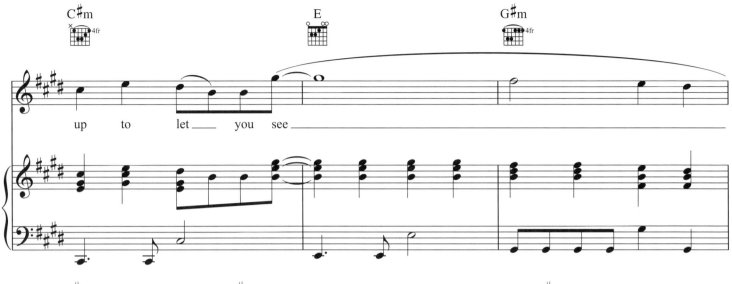

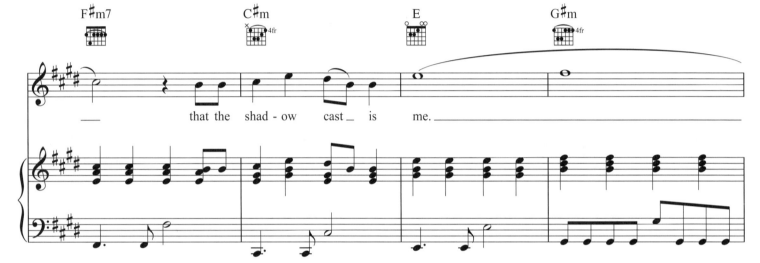

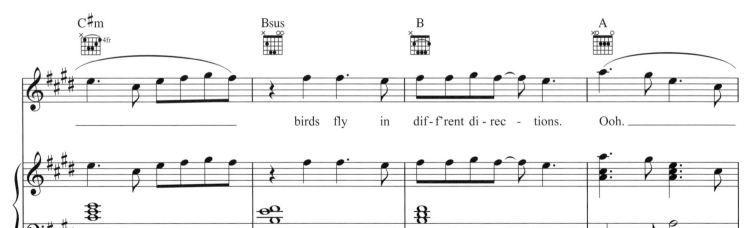

BURN OUT

Words and Music by DAN REYNOLDS,
WAYNE SERMON, BEN McKEE
and DANIEL PLATZMAN

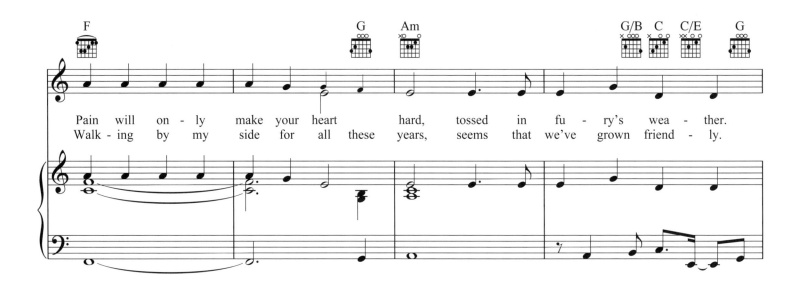

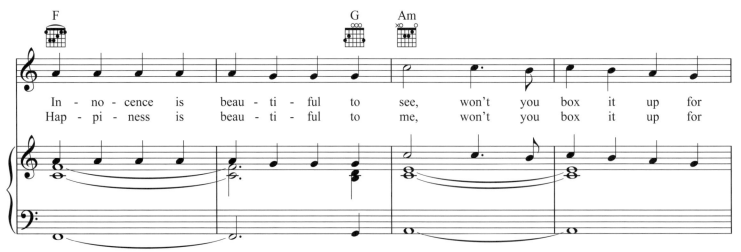

* Recorded a half step higher

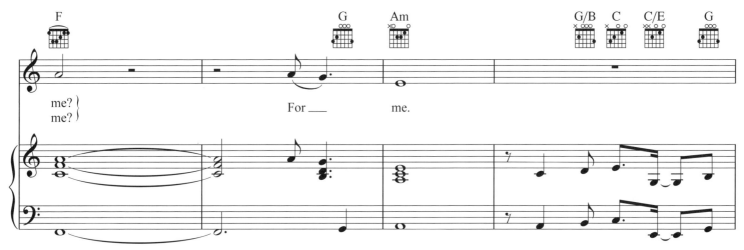

me?
me?
For ___ me.

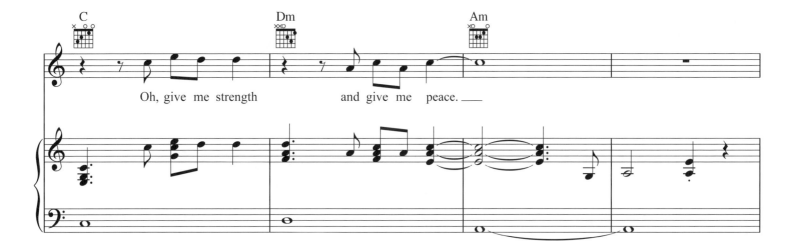

Oh, give me strength ___ and give me peace. ___

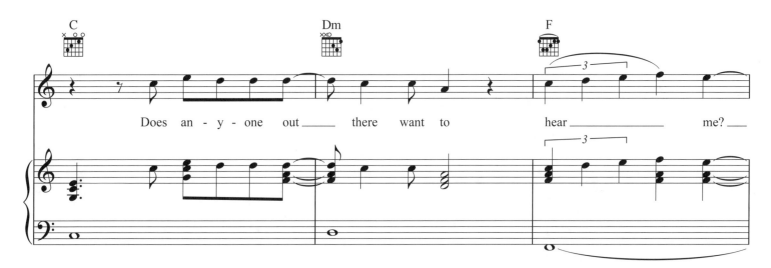

Does an - y - one out ___ there want to hear ___ me? ___

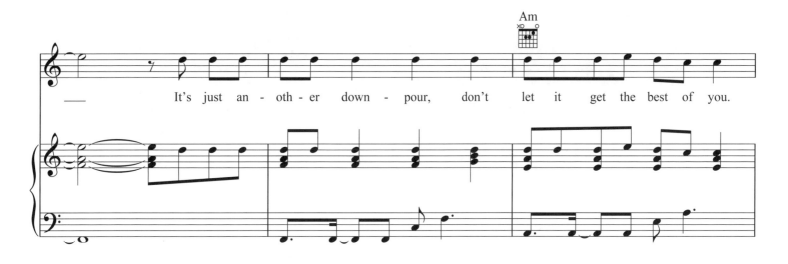

___ It's just an - oth - er down - pour, don't let it get the best of you.

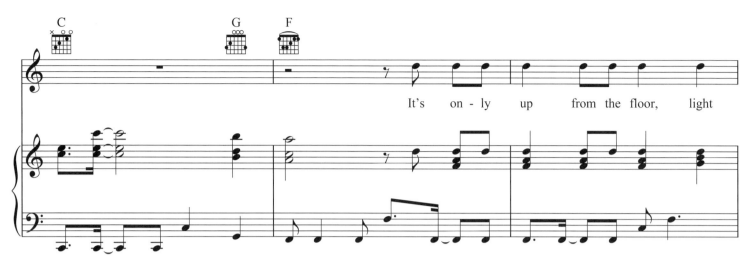

It's on-ly up from the floor, light

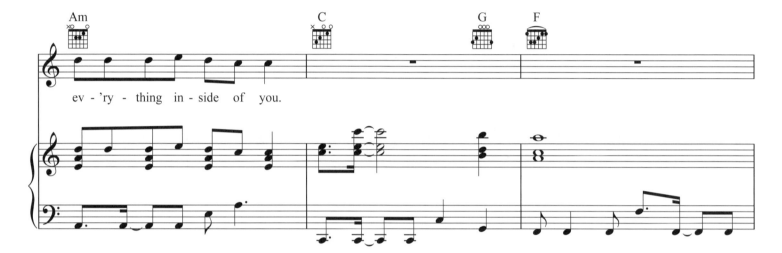

ev-'ry-thing in-side of you.

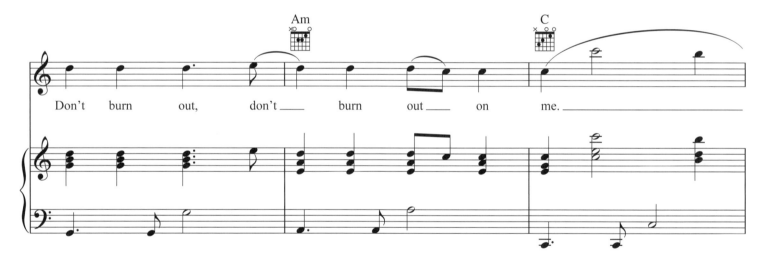

Don't burn out, don't ___ burn out ___ on me. ___

Don't burn out, don't ___ burn out ___ on

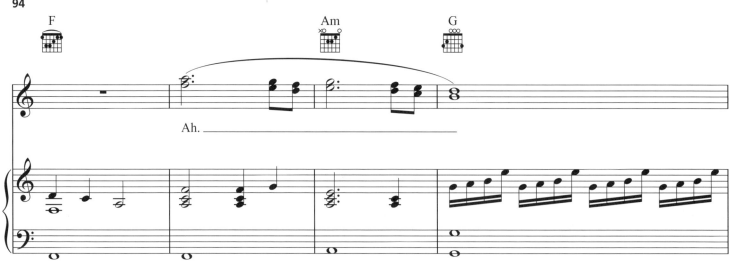

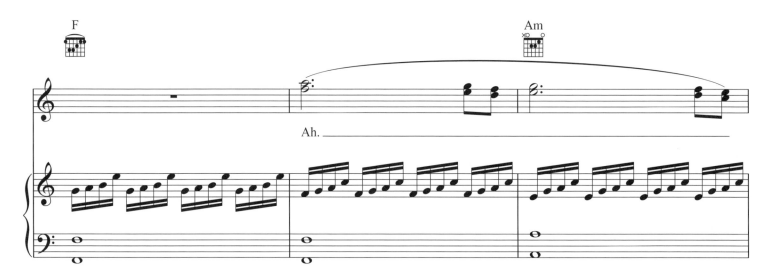

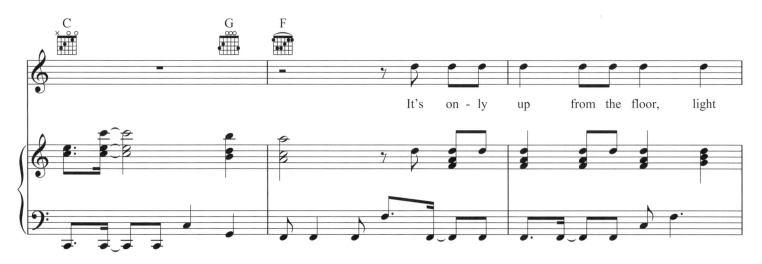

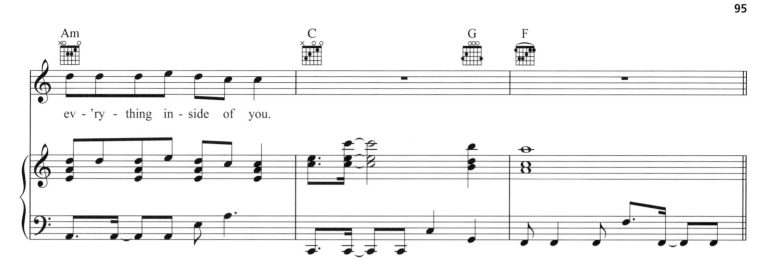

ev - 'ry - thing in - side of you.

I don't want to let you go, I don't want to let you

go. Don't burn out, don't ___ burn out ___ on

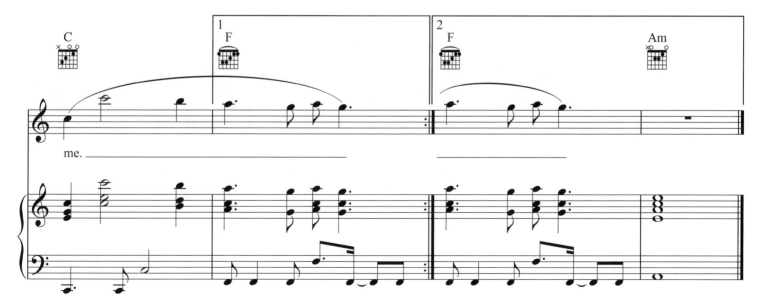

me. ___

REAL LIFE

Words and Music by DAN REYNOLDS,
WAYNE SERMON, BEN McKEE,
DANIEL PLATZMAN and TIM RANDOLPH

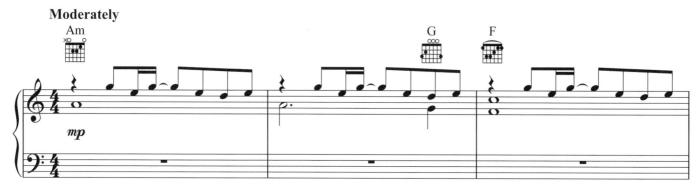

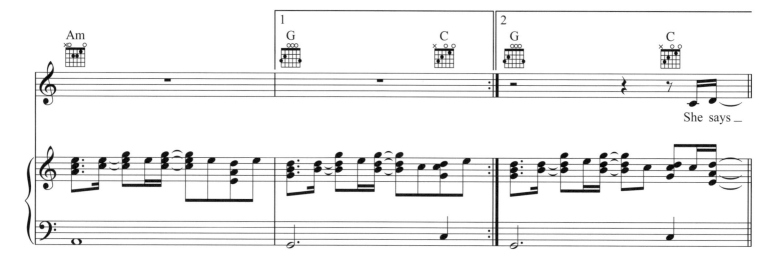

She says

that the world is a bro-ken mess, _____ it's al-ways on _____ her mind. _____

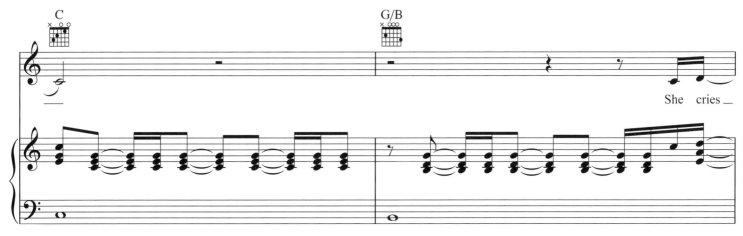

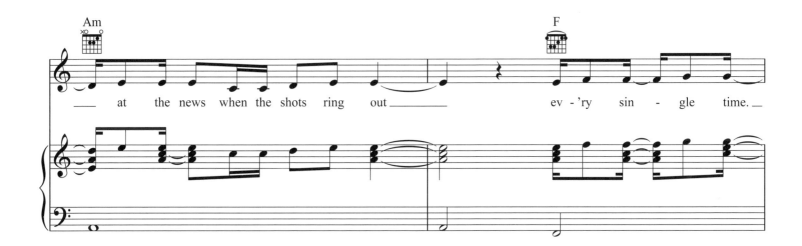

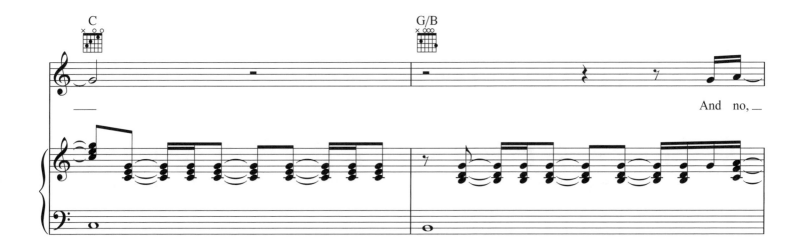

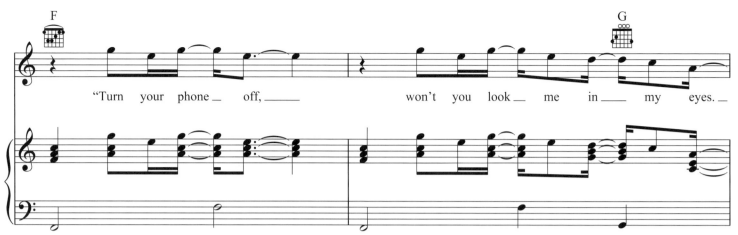

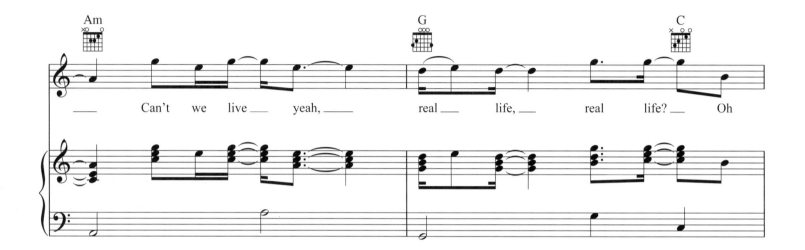

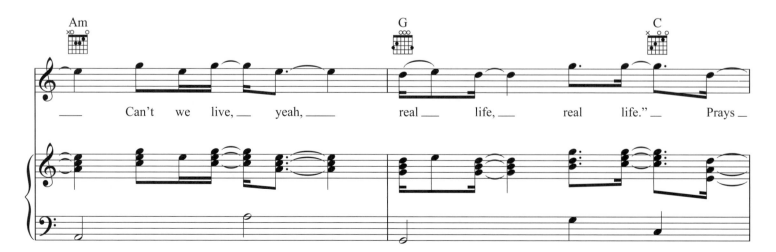

on her knees as the tow - ers fall ___ to a God she does ___ not know.

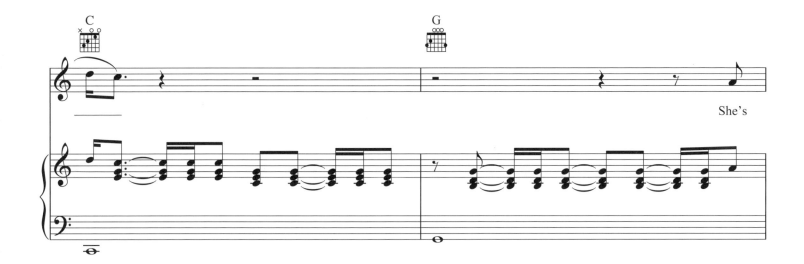

She's

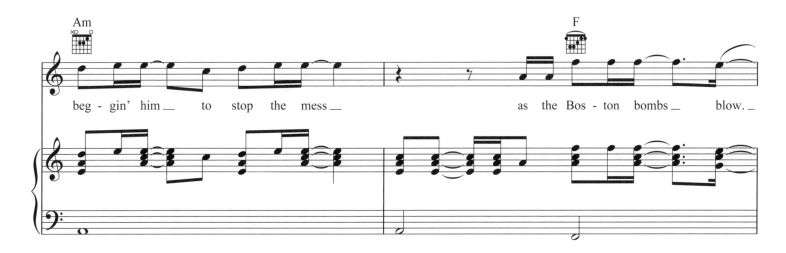

beg - gin' him ___ to stop the mess ___ as the Bos - ton bombs ___ blow.

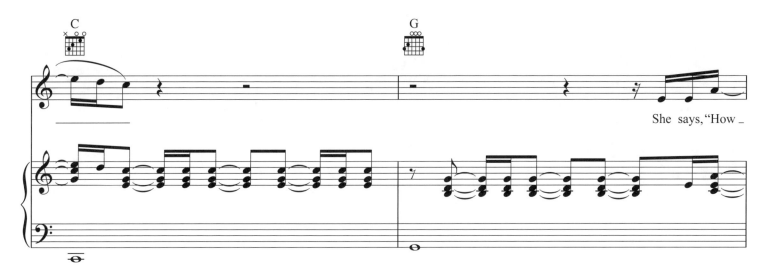

She says, "How ___

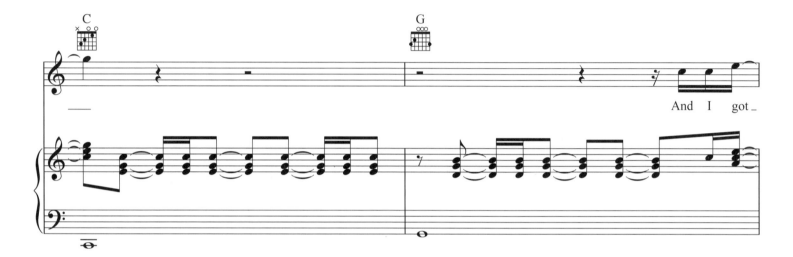

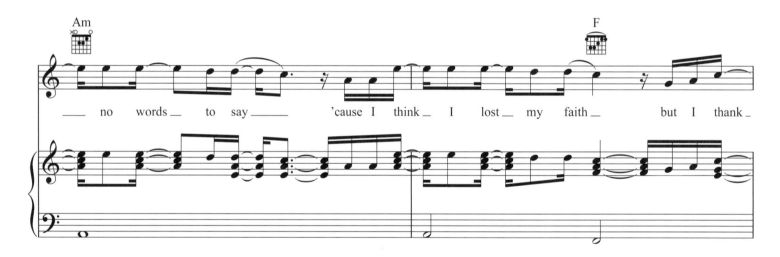

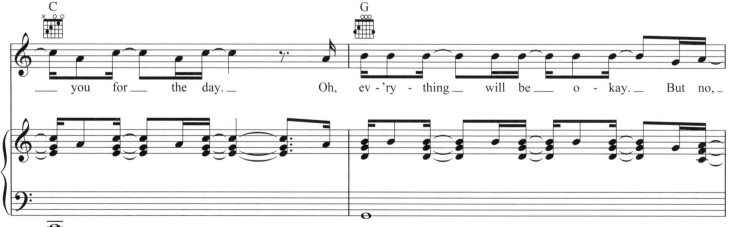

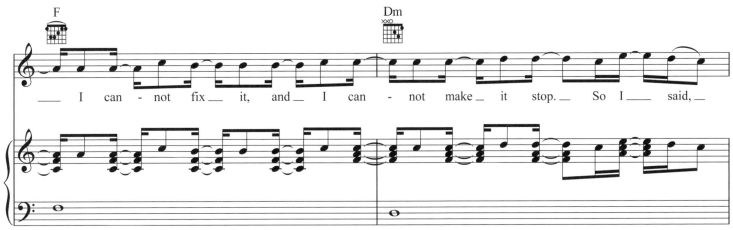

I can-not fix__ it, and__ I can-not make__ it stop.__ So I__ said,__

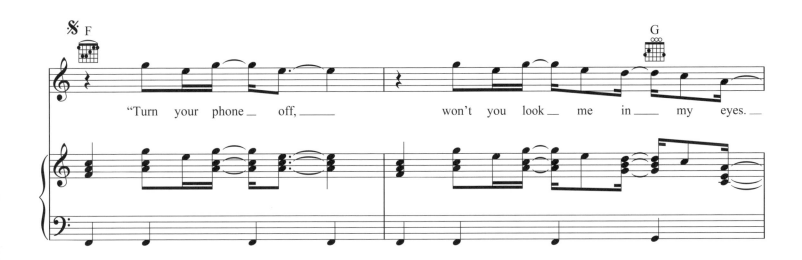

"Turn your phone__ off,_____ won't you look__ me in ___ my eyes.__

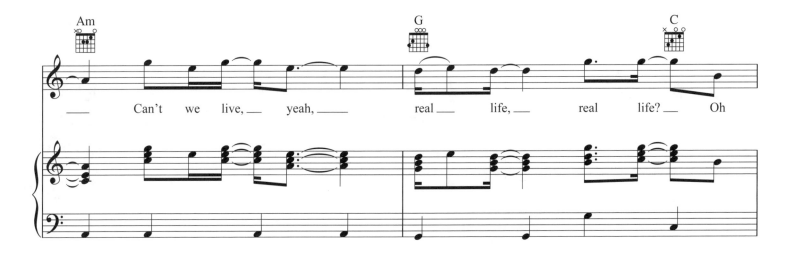

___ Can't we live,__ yeah,_____ real__ life,__ real life?__ Oh

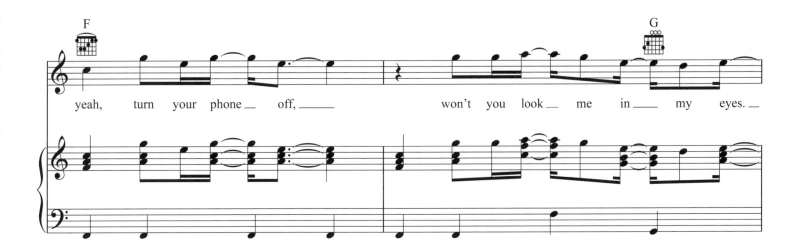

yeah, turn your phone__ off,_____ won't you look__ me in ___ my eyes.__

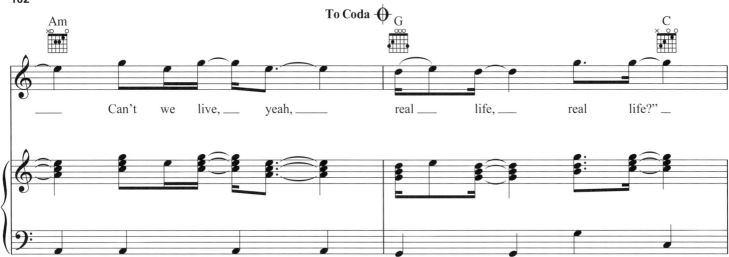

Can't we live, _____ yeah, _____ real _____ life, _____ real _____ life?" _____

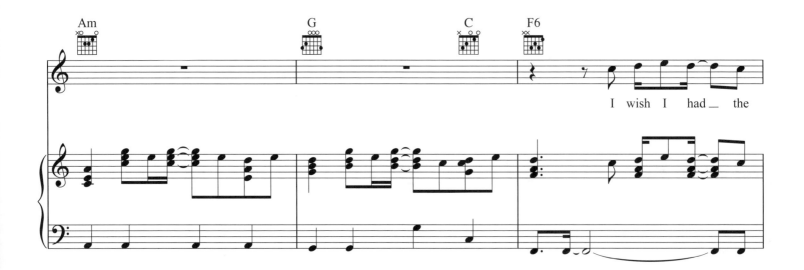

I wish I had __ the

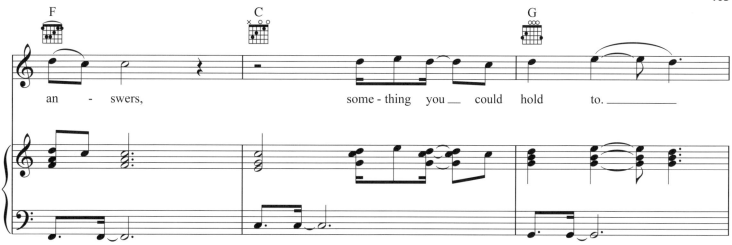

an - swers, some - thing you __ could hold to. __

The on - ly thing __ that's real to me __ is you. __

104

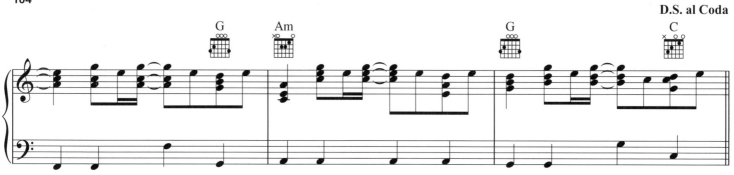

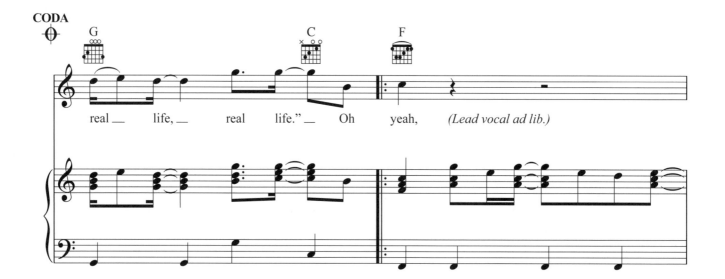

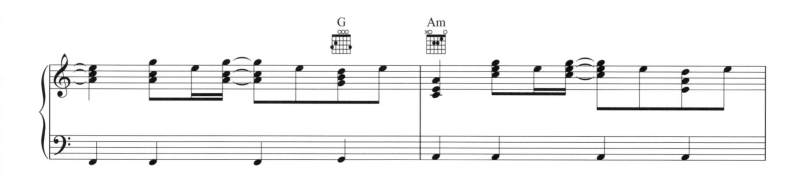

real __ life, __ real life." __ Oh yeah, *(Lead vocal ad lib.)*

real __ life, __ real life. __ Oh yeah.